HOLY ROLLER

ALSO BY DIANNE WILSON

An Unreasonable Woman: A True Story of Shrimpers, Politicos, Polluters, and the Fight for Seadrift, Texas

HOLY ROLLER

GROWING UP IN THE CHURCH OF KNOCK
DOWN DRAG OUT; OR, HOW I QUIT
LOVING A BLUE-EYED JESUS

— A Childhood Memoir —

DIANE WILSON

CHELSEA GREEN PUBLISHING
WHITE RIVER JUNCTION, VERMONT

A NOTE FROM THE AUTHOR

Holy Roller is a memoir of my youth, and as such the events recounted are told from the perspective of a nine- and ten-year-old girl. These events are depicted as I remember them, and that may or may not differ from the perceptions of others, or the reality of circumstances, at the time. In some cases, I have changed names and some personal details to protect the privacy of those mentioned in the book.

Developmental Editor: Joni Praded
Project Manager: Emily Foote
Copy Editor: Robin Catalano
Proofreader: Nancy Ringer
Designer: Peter Holm, Sterling Hill Productions

Printed in the United States of America
First printing, August 2008
10 9 8 7 6 5 4 3 2 1   08 09 10 11 12 13

Our Commitment to Green Publishing

Chelsea Green sees publishing as a tool for cultural change and ecological stewardship. We strive to align our book manufacturing practices with our editorial mission and to reduce the impact of our business enterprise on the environment. We print our books and catalogs on chlorine-free recycled paper, using soy-based inks whenever possible. This book may cost slightly more because we use recycled paper, and we hope you'll agree that it's worth it. Chelsea Green is a member of the Green Press Initiative (www.greenpressinitiative.org), a nonprofit coalition of publishers, manufacturers, and authors working to protect the world's endangered forests and conserve natural resources.

Holy Roller was printed on Natures Book Natural, a 30 percent post-consumer-waste recycled, FSC-certified paper supplied by Thomson-Shore.

Library of Congress Cataloging-in-Publication Data

Wilson, Diane, 1948-
   Holy roller : growing up in the church of knock down drag out, or, How I quit loving
a blue-eyed Jesus / Diane Wilson.
      p. cm.
   ISBN 978-1-933392-82-0
   1. Wilson, Diane, 1948---Childhood and youth. 2. Wilson, Diane, 1948---Family.
3. Seadrift (Tex.)--Biography. 4. Seadrift (Tex.)--Social life and customs--20th century.
5. Seadrift (Tex.)--Rural conditions. 6. Shrimpers (Persons)--Texas--Seadrift. 7. Pentecos-
tals--Texas--Seadrift. 8. Seadrift (Tex.)--Religious life and customs. 9. Environmentalists-
-United States--Biography. 10. Political activists--United States--Biography. I. Title. II.
Title: How I stopped loving a blue-eyed Jesus.

   F394.S4W55 2008
   976.4'121063092--dc22
   [B]
                                                        2008021199
Chelsea Green Publishing Company
Post Office Box 428
White River Junction, VT 05001
(802) 295-6300

www.chelseagreen.com

DEDICATION
To Chief, Billy Bones, and Archie Don.
Wherever you are.

Between living and dreaming there
is a third thing. Guess it.

—ANTONIO MACHADO

HOLY ROLLER

ONE

There were too many girls in too little a space and three of us slept in the same bed and never with me in the middle, but me at the window with my head on the windowsill, where I wrote and scratched out and wrote and scratched out so many messages that there was no paint left on the windowsill. It didn't matter who I wrote to. Jesus. A hay bailer I saw riding on the back end of a truck. Myself, to not backslide into the mud. Or what dream the messages came out of. It just mattered that I wrote. So I wrote, "I will see Jesus in three months."

Now, how did I know that message dropped from heaven and didn't come up from hell? How'd I know that? For Holy Rollers, this was a very important question because you just never knew where the devil abided. Well, I knew because it fell on the third Saturday of the third month with three sisters in the same bed between the hours of nine P.M. to three A.M. (the exact reversed hours Jesus spent on the cross!) and God liked the number 3! Father, Son, and Holy Ghost. Simple simple. God also liked the numbers 7, 12, and 40 but not nearly as much as he liked the number 3. To be absolutely certain, though, I asked Grandma, who was the expert on messages and angels from heaven, and she said it was a sin to dream true dreams. That was witchcraft. Unless, of course, Jesus sent them or sent angels to send them and that was the gift of prophecy. So who did it? The devil or Jesus?

And I said I believed it was Jesus sending angels through my dream doorway.

Grandma said well, she certainly hoped so, because saying Jesus was coming in three months sounded pretty lazy, kinda fishy to her. The Bible said the Rapture was like a thief in the night and a twinkling of the eye and nobody would know so it's best to *always* be prepared. Because how are Holy Ghost people supposed to act? First, last, and every time—waiting on the Rapture! Three months might give saints the idea of a deadline.

Anyhow, Grandma said, that's not to say dreams can't be helpful. Just don't get too familiar with those messenger angels on your own. Don't go hocus-pocus on her. Their home (these dream messenger angels) was the same home as the Father, Son, and Holy Ghost. Yes yes, but also home to Satan and his demons. And you upset their nests and they're liable to swarm down on you like a pile of mean yellow jackets. And I'd seen that, now, ain't I? Yesss ma'am, I had. And these demon yellow jackets attached them-selves to people like ticks on cattle and sucked their juices of human blood and *possessed* them. And even if they're possessed, they don't act like it. No, ma'am. They act like saintly people. Good Christians. Why, some could even speak in tongues and perform minor miracles. Heal the sick, that type of thing. Yes ma'am, they did. So a real help-ful test to see if this saintly person ain't nothing but devil inspired is to ask him to say "Lord Jesus" three times. He can't do it. Now say it, child.

LordJesusLordJesusLordJesus.

Okay, child. You're okay for the minute. Now, this

middle realm. That's the home of palm reading, insanity, and abnormal passions. Don't go there neither.

I wasn't about to go there. I was going to my trusty windowsill to make a running list of the important men in my life. And don't ask me why. I don't know why. It just popped into my head same as that time I decided to write the numbers one to a million on the windowsill and used up all the space. That's why the paint came off. Anyhow, Daddy wasn't on the list because I didn't much care for my daddy at the time, so my Important Man List was a short list and went like this: Jesus, Brother Bob, Abraham Lincoln. Of the living, I loved Brother Bob the best. He was our regular preacher down by the bayou church and was in the middle of going bald.

Now, why I didn't like Daddy.

Momma, Pill (my baby sister), and me tarried (born-again Christian talk meaning "waiting on the Rapture") out back in Quiet Land (our portion of the yard) and Daddy tarried in Secret City (his portion of the yard). When Daddy wasn't out shrimping (and he was always always out shrimping), he was under the pecan tree with a handy cup of coffee, a pack of nasty Camel cigarettes tucked in his pocket, laying marine plywood on the deck of a new boat like he was turning out finished cabinets on Momma's walls. If he wasn't doing that, he was net patching (which took lots and lots of cigarettes). Daddy hunkered over a torn-up, wrecked net spread on the ground, his eyes just slits to keep out all that cigarette smoke and one cigarette after another getting plunked into his mouth. Sometimes an entire ash cigarette hung off his lip! Then the ash cigarette came tumbling down his shirt and he left it there until one of us girls rushed over to brush it off and he'd swat our hands off, saying, Go away. Easy-like, gentle gentle, like a baby watermelon rolling across a sandy field and bumping your hand. Go away.

Momma never knew what Daddy was doing in the front yard because Daddy was a man's man and didn't talk unnecessarily to women, and he had been smoking cigarettes since he was four years old. He also never shut the gate to the henhouse and never touched a farming utensil if he could help it (he was a FISHERMAN) and was a big believer in separating a man's business from a woman's ear. So what net or shrimp boat he was working on or how much it cost or how many boats did that make for him wasn't her business to know. Once Daddy bought a skiff for a price he wouldn't mention and it was hauled into the yard and spent a solid year gathering leaves, and ever' time Momma asked, "Whose that boat out there, Billy?" Daddy said, "Don't know, Goldie. Don't know."

That's why Momma was on the OTHER side of the yard. Daddy had lived in Secret City ever since his Navy days and we had lived in Quiet Land ever since forever. Momma didn't own an electric nothing so she hung clothes on a fishing line tied to a rain cistern where I drew a million Gypsies with long black hair and heart-shaped faces and plunging dresses with tasseled ends and on their arms dozens of bracelets, doodads dripping everywhere, and long, sharp fingernails with nickel-sized ruby rings on at last three, maybe four fingers.

I drew interesting-looking men, too. Hay bailers with long hair hiding their eyes and strong, dusty arms to turn hay and deckhands who drifted into town off boats from faraway places like Terrebonne Parish in Louisiana or Port Bolivar across from Galveston. And everyone wearing boots. Rattlesnake boots, alligator boots, boots with shooting stars, toe-peeled boots, unraveled and busted-out boots. Sometimes I drew them wearing rubber boots just like my daddy.

I know, I know, I was a hypocrite and a confused little girl but I was nine and not thirteen (the Age of Accountability and God's line in the sand saying, Old enough to know better) so I wasn't shooting to hell just yet. I was four years short of shooting to hell and like the perilous beginnings of all great descents, little boxes need to stack up before little boxes can fall down. Anyhow, Pill was disrupting my evil drawings a dozen times with a made-up song about baby Moses floating down the Nile and she sang it so loud and long that her voice went hoarse, and I knew and Momma knew that Pill would sing the bark off a fence post so to shut her up some Momma said, "Save it for the missionaries next Sunday, baby." (Momma always called her "baby" like she was two years old and the cutest part in the Christmas play.)

Holy Rollers loved missionaries. Hey, I loved missionaries too. They were the generals in God's army! That's why I was a Junior Missionette (girls nine to twelve years old). Missionettes always met on Sunday evening right before the night church service so we could get from one church thing to the next church thing without indulging in any worldly nonsense like riding around in cars and chewing gum. We all wore the same Missionette uniform too. White shirt (purity and submission), navy blue skirt (labor for the Lord), and a little gold pin (golden streets of glory), stamped *M* in the middle and pinned to our shoulder. We'd sit around a metal table in an empty part of the church—ten little girls number-painting Jesus's face in oil and eating vanilla wafers and drinking red Kool-Aid until our lips were red as a horde of Jezebels. We had a huge responsibility on our little white shoulders: just by sitting there we were setting good examples and winning souls to Christ and it was unfortunate that nobody could see us.

After the Jesus faces and the Kool-Aid ran out, the pastor's wife lined us up to test our memories on books of the Bible. My limit was about seven. I'd go straight for the easy ones: Matthew, Mark, Luke, and John. Then I'd hop over to what I called the devil chapters: Deuteronomy and Revelation. Finally, I gave up with the easiest one of all: Genesis.

My momma was a serious serious Christian woman with two preachers in the family and a mother who obsessed over a radio evangelist from San Antonio. But her emphasis was cleanliness was godliness and no body part was too low to be in service, so she wasn't much for batting books of the Bible around with her kids. That was a huge waste of time! She could have two lines of wash strung out before the pastor's wife said Deuteronomy or Ecclesiastes. So the same girl won every time and the pastor's wife always handed her the same prize: a scrapbook full of pictures of Christians wearing heavy coats at a revival somewhere in Alaska. We didn't know who they were.

Being a Junior Missionette didn't take up all my time. There was leftover time for the Gypsy drawing. There was leftover time for the windowsill messages. Then there was time for hiding. But almost as good as the hiding was seeing how long I could sleep in the middle of the road before a truck came. So far I had made it six days without nothing major happening except the sun coming out from behind a cloud and blistering me. I was a fierce little bump in the road, as any truck driver would tell you

Anyhow, hiding I did best and I was hiding under the kitchen table and Momma was slaving away over the stove and burning the fish when Sister Pearl shot into the kitchen and shouted, "Praise Jesus, Sister Goldie! The missionaries are comin'!"

Sister Pearl was a big German lady with a white crepe face and neck and she had more hair than me and Momma put together and always wore it pinned up around her head like a crown of thorns. She was also a big housecleaning fool with a huge farmhouse with lots of rooms and front and back porches and an attic that needed cleaning from top to bottom and behind boards nailed to the walls and underneath iron bathtubs and in pitch-black closets, so I was watching her shoes and hoping she'd scoot right back to her farmhouse. But she leaned down and peeked under the table like she'd seen me just yesterday fooling around with the worst boys in town. "You know, Silver, Jesus can see you under there. You can't hide from Jesus."

Well, I wasn't hiding from Jesus, but you just never know. No telling where the devil abided. My thinking cap ain't on straight sometimes. Also, too many girls in a house can lead to sisters getting confused for their sisters, so maybe Sister Pearl meant Jesus was spying on Sheena. Did she mean

Sheena? Jesus certainly had lots more interesting things to see with Sheena. But I figured it was me. Wicked wicked me drawing evil Gypsy Jezebels with red fingernail polish on the rain cistern. So I hung out my bottom lip more than I normally did until Sister Pearl said, "Jesus is gonna trip on that bottom lip if you ain't careful, honey."

If I'd had any wits I'd have realized that Sister Pearl was just missionary shopping. She was a member of the Women's Missionary Council that met every Wednesday morning and Sunday evening and they were always scouting for missionary-type girls for God's Army because Satan never played fair and his evil forces were out all the time trying to tempt little girls. So recruitment was critical. And for a missionary scout like Sister Pearl, there was absolutely nothing worse than the devil sliding in with a pout and ruining a perfectly good missionary candidate.

But I didn't have wits. Wits were a Sheena thing. I was into emotional flip-flopping as fast as I could. I was a regular roller coaster. Faster faster! Drive Momma crazy. Drive Daddy crazy. JesusJesusJesus one second, then the next second *whomp*, lying in middle of the road or hanging by my toes from a high, slick chinaberry limb in the front yard to see how long I could stay there until my toes gave out. I had been hanging about ten minutes, focusing mightily on my steely toes, when Sister Pearl drove into Momma's yard in her blue shark-fin car rimmed in silver chrome and before she could say *boo* I fell to her feet from high in the chinaberry tree.

I was sprawled in the oyster dust, watching the chinaberry tree watch me, not saying a word 'cause words ain't necessary when you fall on your head. Words won't describe it. Say the word and that ain't it. A little electrical storm drummed across my feet like hail pinging a still bay. *Pingpingpingpingping. PONG!* Suddenly I was cleaning Jesus's house and he was reading the obituary column, seeing who was dead and where their folks were and who was surviving that family, and he already had the phone sitting in his lap with pencil marks on the paper and the receiver at his ear.

How many times you sinned? he asked, and I said three, and he asked, What are they?

Well, I had to think a minute. Stick on my thinking cap. That first time the second-grade class had an Easter party and the whole class was invited to the picture show in town and we all paraded single-file down the road swinging our arms and stirring up oyster dust with our feet. Then we sat in a dark theater and watched Anthony Perkins, dressed up like an Indian, slip into the swamp and disappear. He was carrying something. Bird feathers? A baby? I don't remember. He just disappeared and that was the end. The whole time, though, I expected the Rapture to commence with me sitting in a picture show.

That second time, I was standing under the chinaberry tree (the same tree I just fell out of in the front yard) and the words *damndamndamndamn* came into my head as easy as pie and wouldn't shut off for days. Drove me flat nuts! *Damndamndamndamndamn*. Like that!

Then the third time our neighbor Ticky (he later took an ax to his brother, but at the time he was living nicely down in the pasture with him) went to California to bat tennis balls around and he came back with a box of women's silky underwear and lounging pajamas and when he dropped them off in Momma's kitchen, I had a screaming fit with my sisters over some red leotards.

Jesus looked down at the obituary column, then back up at me. His eyes were pitifully sad. "That doesn't sound too good. Now, which kid of Goldie's are you?"

"The middle one," I said.

"And how old?"

"Nine," I said.

"Oh, you're too young, then."

I wasn't dead after all. So for that "not dead" reason, plus her own missionary agenda, Sister Pearl said, "Praise Jesus! This baby's beat death to be a missionary in the Congo. It's a sign. A miracle. Thank you, Jesus."

She was right, you know. Besides Gypsy drawings and toe hangings and lying in the middle of the road, I was dough on anybody's dough board. I was missionary dough on Sister Pearl's dough board and nurse dough on Momma's dough board. Momma was a born-again Christian but big big on nursing. Her dream for a short while was to be a nurse but she got married and, BOOM!, had seven kids instead, so she transferred her aborted nursing dream onto her daughters. It was a tangled, twisted little fetus of a thing. Never quite living, not quite dead. But no matter, the nursing dream was like a possum up a tree and she was the kid with a stick trying to hit it over the head; she never hit it squarely on the head, but ever' time she thought about it, she went out and took another swing at it.

Momma had lived all her life in one little town and had

never went beyond the city-limit sign until she was about twenty-five, when she and her three kids rode on a train to Clute, Texas, to visit an uncle. By nightfall the uncle wanted to know when she and that batch of kids was leaving, so Momma left Clute and went home crying. She never left again. Momma said the only reason a woman needed to be outta the house was if she was making money and if she was a woman she wasn't making much so really there wasn't no reason for her to be outta the house. Unless she was a nurse. Nurses made lots of money. So Momma wanted every one of us girls to be a nurse and hardly one of us was heading that way, so Momma ran out of ideas on what to do with us besides sending us to church. Maybe one of us would be a missionary. Sacrifice and money. Momma was big on one and knew a lot about the scarcity of the other. So make lots of money or go to the Congo as a missionary and get hacked to pieces and buried in a shoebox. (No missionary made it alive out of the Congo.)

But in the beginning, I was even too much for Sister Pearl, the missionary hunter. I had no personality. I didn't talk. I had an odd habit of lying in the middle of the road. I certainly wasn't Sister Pearl's favorite pick to clean her house because I never let out a peep about what was going on in our house or what my other three aunts were saying and all their kids were doing. Kids that didn't talk and tell stories about what was going on in the house was no fun for Sister Pearl. How was she to know anything? Later on, though, Sister Pearl decided not talking wasn't so bad. It was a good quality for missionaries. Who needed a complaining missionary?

In Sister Pearl's book, a missionary was the highest calling Jesus gave out. It beat the brother passing around the collection plate, it beat the deacon, it even tied with the preacher and, in terms of sacrifice, it beat the preacher. And for plenty reasons. Missionaries were all about sacrifice and no fun. Fun was the devil. Fun would lead you astray. Fun would lead you down the woolly mammoth path of iniquity. So consequently, missionaries were dead serious and did dull things like die. (Whoosh, off with their heads and bury them in a shoebox.)

So when the missionaries finally came to town (just like Sister Pearl prophesized) it was strongly advised that nobody mess with them. No foolish words. NO JOKING! A mighty spooky time for everybody where even the cedar trees made the most mournful *whooh whoooh* and the waves crashed on the shore and the graveyard—oh, that was a mighty dangerous place to go.

The sisters in the church did lots of cooking in preparation for the missionaries' arrival: soft simmering gumbo with shrimp and tender okra and fresh tomatoes hand-plucked from the garden and dewberries from the pasture. Nothing too harsh for those saintly mouths! The brothers hauled shrimp from the bay, then stood outside the church (they were fishermen and just traded their fishing pants and boots for dark pants and shoes and white long-sleeved shirts), and ever' now and then they slipped back in, quiet and respectful, through the side screen door to make sure the sisters didn't need some more shrimp hauled in. Then they left without saying a word or bumping into anybody unnecessarily.

Then the pastor rounded up the mommas and told them to keep their kiddies home tonight. The true but horrific stories coming out of the mouths of the missionaries might terrify them. Better to just send the Missionettes. Those little soldiers of Christ. So the Missionettes were stuck on the front row at the Church of Jesus Loves You and I was nine and a Missionette so I was stuck there, too.

Then the Jesus crowd piled in and oh, glory hallelujah, it was an exciting time. Not nearly as exciting as the Rapture, but close—close. The band was doing its best to keep up— playing guitar, fiddle, bass fiddle, banjo, and tambourine to every gospel song they knew plus venturing into a little something the guitar player's first cousin played with a country western band. And wasn't it just too bad that country western band wasn't swiping through Corpus on a bus tour 'cause then that cousin might just show up, duded up and decked out in his black pants and black Western shirt with the long fringes. Then he'd show the crowd! He'd do some real fancy picking on his electric guitar plugged into a huge black box.

Normally band qualifications were pretty slim, so anybody with guts enough to play something or sing something was welcome to get up there and try. And if the Holy Ghost anointed you, why, that was even better. Get on up there! What are you sitting down for? Usually a sister or two would get up and harmonize on a song they'd made up that morning, and once a prickly haired boy with a banged-up trumpet that he couldn't get a note from because he said he'd washed the horn in soapsuds that morning to get rid of some old spit. Another time a brother (clearly a Yankee or why else was he wearing that floppy corduroy hat?) hit two clattering spoons on his knee. What a treat! A first time for everything.

Hopefully, the Holy Ghost had arrived. Hopefully, he was present and hovering, but if he wasn't, he certainly needed to be invited in. Somebody needed to do something. So the band started playing a victory march and the brothers and the sisters in Christ joined hands, going round and round the chairs, praising Jesus, hurrahing for the Holy Ghost, and laughing when they whacked their hips against a chair 'cause they weren't feeling any pain. You don't feel any pain when you're waaay above it all and headed for Canaan's Fair Land. Only the older sisters and brothers who couldn't get on their feet easily and the mommas with tiny babies were excused from the victory march, but even then some got up and cripped around, shouting, "Better to wear out than to rust out!"

Being a missionary-type girl and terribly shy, I wasn't much for front-row anything so I scooted back to the mid-row seats where Momma was sitting with Sister Pearl. Momma was holding a worn Bible from the house in her lap and a paper fan Sister Pearl had given her and she was whacking the air so fast I could hardly see her face. WHAM WHAM WHAM. Between the fan's whacking and the holy-rolling dancing, Sister Pearl clapped her hands and tapped her foot and ever' now and then she reached over and patted my leg, saying, "My little missionary."

Behind the band, a black-haired evangelist sat on a three-seat section of folding chairs and cleaned his fingernails. He was waiting his turn. Sister Pearl leaned over and whispered in my ear, "He's just fillin' in for Brother Bob while he's workin' in Seguin, honey."

Well, I knew that already 'cause Sister Pearl ironed ever' stitch of his clothes after he arrived in town, same as me and Sheena ironed ever' stitch of hers while she stood and watched from the kitchen door to make sure we did it right. It didn't make sense what she did. Iron his. Don't iron yours. But I was nine and clearly I didn't understand evangelists. Evangelists probably had wives. Maybe they did. There was nothing that said they couldn't have wives. They just didn't *need* wives. Not when there were women in the church to wash and iron their clothes, feed them home-cooked meals, and give them downtime with nobody to bother them. In return all they had to do was liven up a dead church with tongue speaking, a little jumping, dancing, singing glory hallelujah, saving the sinners, and resaving the backsliders. And maybe, Jesus willing, a little miracle. Tonight it was double our pleasure with the missionaries and the evangelists all on the same night. It was like a comet from heaven coming through with both ends lit.

Normally, evangelists came once a month. That's why they were called *visiting* evangelists. And it was always on a Sunday and never on a Wednesday 'cause Wednesday was waaay too quiet for them. Unless, of course, the church was really, really dead and then they came down for a solid week of revival. Tent revivals. Brush arbors. Evangelizing on the back end of a truck bed. It didn't matter. Getting sinners to the altar was the trick. So a truck drove around town with speakers mounted on the hood and announced that a mighty outpouring of the Holy Ghost was coming to the Church of Jesus Loves You, Monday through Sunday night. Come one, come all, and get yourself saved at the altar.

During revivals, the evangelists' impatience, which was normally short anyhow, revved up about ten notches. They were really impatient now. Sitting on a chair would make them twitch. Sitting on a chair would make them feel like slapping something. We called it the Holy Ghost jitters and it made preachers hop up and down the aisle, jump on the altar, whoop it up around the church like an Indian, slap the Bible against their skinny leg, or—the best money for the buck—slap the pulpit with the Bible. That sounded like a shrimp boat hitting the wharf and taking off half the docks. It was electrifying! The air filled with shouts and strange lights waffled in and out of the church rafters. It was just like on Pentecost when a mighty wind blew and twelve beacons of fire danced above the heads of the twelve apostles.

The black-headed evangelist got up and walked to the pulpit. He said he was gonna say a little prayer first and after that a deacon (Brother Tom, who was perched on the edge of a chair and waiting) would pass around a plate for a love offering for the missionaries.

He prayed, "Help us, Lord. God bless the poor sinner in here today. The backslider, the unregenerate, the drunkard, the derelict, these church members, these emissaries from the Congo. They're here, Lord, because they know that Jesus saves. But so does Satan. The devil believes and trembles before Jesus's precious name. When Satan attacks, the Comforter says Jesus Jesus Jesus. Demons recoil when they hear his single name. So, God, be merciful with us today. We're just your humble servants. In Jesus's name we ask it. Amen."

Next he wanted to welcome the Lord's heavenly born soldiers who had been fighting their way through the battlefield of good and evil in the Congo. "Brothers and sisters," he said, "looky here at this fiiine missionary couple. These here little baby angel missionary kids. Saints, ain't no baby too small for Jesus. He says if you got knees you can pray. These here folks are the flaming torches in darkest Aferker. Just recently they were a hair's breath—with hatchets whooping over their heads—and saints, that's French for 'being killed'! Killed by the Mau Mau tribes in that heathen nation. Oh, precious Jesus looking down on us here tonight, open our eyes. Because what does it tell us in the Bible? Greater love hath no man than this that he laid down his life for his friend. Yeeesss, Lord . . . these folks here. Sacrifice! That's just what we're talking about! Sacrifice sacrifice sacrifice. They've been laying their lives under a sharp hatchet so those heathen folks over there can get a chance to be washed in the precious blood of the lamb, just like me and you here tonight. Sacrifice, brothers and sisters. And that sacrifice is for y'all too. It's not just for them over in that heathen continent—no! Y'all too. 'Cause remember, folks, the Lord cannot return. He will be delayed until these distant dark places hear the *true* message. Until the Pentecostal flame is in Canada and an outpouring is felt in Central America and a mighty shock of power hits Egypt. Kapowee! Get me a machine gun for Jesus! In America too, brothers and sisters. Kapowee! Kapowee! Get me *two* machine guns for Jesus! We need the old-time religion back! The camp meetings, the revivals, the mission work, the street and prison work. Getting folks to accept Christ and speak in tongues, getting glories untold. If they do that, then legally they *will* go to Heaven. They *will* get glories untold. Same as every man, woman, and child who rejects Jesus, declaring his suffering pointless, must legally go to hell. Regardless of God's feelings about you. You *must* go to hell.

"Saints, this True Message—and I'm not talking that mumbo jumbo mess you hear from the Baptist or the Methodist across the street—the ONLY gospel that will establish the Lord's kingdom worldwide is the full gospel message known and preached ONLY by the Pentecostals. What is preached here tonight, brothers and sisters. Praise Jesus and bring on the Rapture!"

The evangelist said he figured three hundred million (three Raptures at a hundred million apiece) of the Pentecostal believers that were ready and still on the warpath for Jesus would go straight up. Soon as that event took place, the Great Tribulation (which might last seven years or several thousand years because it was God's ultimate instrument for convincing sinners to mend their ways and who knows how long that would take) would commence. None of the "ordinary Christians" such as Baptists, Methodists, and such—bogged down, no doubt, by worldly concerns (money, houses, cars, boats, stocks, and such)—would make it out. And forget that Cult of Mary! They used confession as a way to sin even more. That ungodly horde of priests, nuns, brothers, bishops, cardinals, and POPE (don't forget the pope, chief devil) would perish in the fires of the Great Deceiver.

DOOMSDAY was certainly entertaining and mainly because I was safe beside Momma. We were caught like rocks in Jesus's sandal, so wherever he trod, we trod too. I could hang by my toes as long as I wanted. The grave wasn't for me.

Momma was fidgeting beside me. Oh, I knew my momma well. She didn't want a near date. No sudden Rapture. She had a million chores to do. She wished she were home. She wished those preachers would just shorten those sermons. But Momma's wishing wasn't in charge tonight. Nope, she was sitting there just like the rest of us, tarrying on the Holy Ghost who wandered wherever he wanted to go. As the evangelist said, "If you're sitting in a church and you know every step the Holy Ghost is fixing to make, then you're sitting in a backslidden church!"

Well, the Holy Ghost was riding tall in his saddle tonight and nobody was bringing him down or telling him what to do. The evangelist started running around the altar with the Bible up to his chest, then he stopped and slammed the Bible on the altar like he just whacked an escaping roach. Somebody hollered, "Jeesssus's blood blood blood blood." Two sisters sitting on an end row were obviously under the heat of the Holy Ghost fire and they stood up, scooted past some brothers and sisters, then walked up front and stood with the band. They had identical long hair and long skirts and their faces were white as bedsheets with eyeholes cut out. Overhead the fan rocked a little and sent flickering waves of heat from the rafters, and a light on the ceiling slid down the arms of the missionary couple. We were blessed! The Holy Ghost fire was hovering.

The sisters were regular singers and had enough singing talent that they could've easily been on the Louisiana Hay Ride and on TV if they wanted to. But they didn't want to. They'd turned their lives over to Jesus and they believed they would sing a little song if the Holy Ghost would allow it and if the brothers there would play a little guitar for them. So under heaven's hole and under the hot lights, the sisters lifted their faces and sang: "Greeateeer luuuv hath nooo man than thisss, that heee laid dooowwwn hiiis life for hiiis frieeend."

Then the first sister slumped over and down came the second sister, *WHAM WHAM*. They were slain in the spirit. Collapsing in the abiding arms of the Lord. But to me they just died. Dead as a hammer.

Oh, help me, Lord. Save me, Jesus!

TWO

Momma's pregnancies were hellacious. First she vomited her guts out and then she cried about it. If that wasn't enough to cement the connection between hell and pregnancy, six months into her fourth pregnancy, while hanging out a washtub of wet clothes on a line tied to a rain cistern where rats and birds fell plus we got our water, a blood clot froze in her eyes and she went blind in one. One-eyed and one year later, Momma had me. (Nothing slowed down her baby train.) It was October, the dead-last phase of the moon, and summerlike with the windows open but screened to keep out the mosquitoes that were always worse after dark. I was delivered, howling like a banshee, in my grandma's bed by Aunt Teny, whose curly, frizzy hair mine eventually resembled.

I was not the first grandkid born at Grandma's but the fifth. And while babies might have started at home, they always ended up at Grandma's because she had an indoor toilet and many helpful girls: Goldie Belle, Silver, Tena Perlina (Teny), and June Bug. (Grandma had attempted to name all her girls after precious jewels mentioned in the Bible, but she quit and settled on a month of the year for the youngest girl because a neighbor lady said Garnet sounded like Jezebel.) Grandma had a couple of taboos on childbearing. One, don't mention that nasty word! But if you must, then call it PG. Two, a woman's insides would fall out if she set foot on the floor too soon after delivery so for two solid weeks, Grandma and her three girls waited on Momma hand and foot (this was the only time Momma was queen of anything), and in the evening fried chicken and dumplings and biscuits in a covered skillet were toted from the bayou house (where Grandma and the girls were) to the shinnery house (where Daddy and the boys were).

Then Daddy showed up from shrimping one day and, lo and behold, there was a new screaming baby in the house. Daddy was indifferent to the whole baby thing and the most he'd do was put one rubber fishing boot against the baby's butt and say, "Goldie, this baby's diaper needs changing." Only once was a baby (my brother) delivered in Momma's iron bed and for once Daddy got to see the whole messy little affair from scratch and in her delirium Momma called Daddy Billy Bones, which she never did again.

Most screaming babies take a couple days to calm down, a month at the most, but I never calmed down. I screamed like I had a hot poker stuck to my foot—until I didn't. And I stopped because I was sent to Houston to visit my curly-haired Aunt Teny (who had only one kid) and I fell in love with their cement sidewalk. Momma thought it was the 150-mile ride that ended the crying, but it wasn't. The cement sidewalk did it.

The cement-sidewalk love affair was cut short, though, 'cause Daddy liked all his kids in one spot and not farmed out (for a starving fisherman, he had an inordinate amount of pride), so I was sent home to Momma, who had two more babies, and my fascination with cement was transferred to a baby bottle that I sucked until I was four. I didn't see my Aunt Teny again until a hurricane sent an open invitation to her and her feisty union husband and her one kid: come to Seadrift and live with Grandma in the Land of Plenty. Which was exactly what they did. They moved from Houston to Grandma's bayou house that had shifted off its blocks in a storm and left them a leaning metal bed to sleep in.

If Aunt Teny's husband had a horse he would have rode it out of town quick because Seadrift was a town that had no love of union men. She only loved fishermen. But he didn't have a horse so he got over it soon enough and set up a store that for nine long years was a Main Street attraction along with a picture show, a dry goods store where unsold clothes hung so long on the racks that the sun rotted the seams, and a Western Auto store where fishermen bought rope, shackles, and webbing with promises of payment come a good shrimp season.

I was sitting (hiding) in Uncle Bill's empty potato bin and not because I was scared of Uncle Bill who cussed on a dime, shouting, "You demon, you demon! I'm gonna keeel you!" if you messed with one iota of anything of his; I was hiding because crying had wore my young life out and hiding was the extent of my projection into the world. And anything would make me hide. I hid because the sun came up funny. I hid because of a bad dream. I hid because somebody said I had a big bottom lip and did I play the trumpet? Did I pout a lot? Once I hid because my brother burned my paper dolls that I'd cut from a Sears catalog and had propped up on a pillow with a quilt covering their paper legs.

And the potato bin wasn't the first place I'd hid, it was just the latest. I hid in weeds and in ankle-deep mud with foam nearly in my nose, and sometimes I hid in an old wrecked car in the pasture and watched a million yellow jackets track across the blurred windows and beat their wasp wings like Momma's finger beating against my chest. You listening to me, Silver? You listening to me? Well, one part was and one part wasn't and the part that wasn't, Momma said, was one queer girl. One time I hid in a high leafy branch overhanging the only road in front of our house and a man on a tractor came by, looked up, saw my funny little face, and nearly ran into the ditch. Another time I was underneath Momma's bed and I forget who all was left in the bedroom while Momma was pulling off her Sunday dress, but Pill was warting the fool out of the cat hiding under the bed with me.

Pill leaned down and her voice cracked when she bent over. She said, "Whooo do you luuuv, Siiilvaaah? Whooo do you luuuv?"

I grabbed the yellow cat lying in the dust and shouted, "I love Jesus and Brother Bob! And Abraham Lincoln!"

Momma yelled, "Leave her alone!" and Pill said, "Whyyy?" And Momma said, *"You know."* That's what Momma said: *"You know."*

Well, half the *you know* was five women in the same house with one having a whole room to herself while three slept in the same bed with the one nearest the window hiding and taking notes on the windowsill. Of the three sisters in the same bed, Sheena was the cleverest, the oldest, and the prettiest (Pill was just the cutest) and she liked conflict as much as Momma hated it and I disappeared before it arrived. For instance, in the cold early-morning hours after a howling norther blew the leaves off every tree and shoved half the water from the bay, Sheena tossed us out of bed just to rearrange the quilts and the pillows and the sheets. She was boss of the bed. Any questions? Any takers? Well, not Pill, who just grogged around, saying, "Ughhh." A real deadhead seeking warmth. Even a thimbleful. So half the time she ended up curled in a knot on the floor while I ticked away in silence and devised a bomb for Sheena's fat head. A big ax to fall on her big fat skull. Finally she told me to go back to my spot at the window. And I did.

Sheena was twelve years old and every boy cousin we had (we had six) was in love with her. She was as sophisticated as it was gonna get at her age and living in the country like we did. (My oldest sister's, Nina's, level exceeded all our expectations. She was sixteen, had a room to herself, and possessed a huge can of perfumed talcum powder that she got as a graduation present and for being so smart and she used it on every nook and cranny in her body and in the process drenched the floor, the walls, and a cedar hope chest where a half dozen of Grandma's string rugs and one crocheted white-shell afghan nestled until the D-day of her marriage.) After Momma hid Ticky's box of California underwear out behind the cow shed to keep us girls from rushing headlong into prostitution or Jezebel-style dressing, Sheena was the first to find the box, cut off one of the black silky nighties up to her bum, then swing through the trees, calling herself Sheena, Queen of the Jungle.

Sheena had already jumped off the bayou bridge, been inside a domino hall, been outside a carnival tent, and was the proud owner of a velvet painting of two wineglasses and a smoking cigarette that the guy behind the carnival tent got in Mexico and gave her and she shoved under our bed and Daddy found and slashed with Momma's paring knife. On Sunday evenings when Sheena was supposed to be in church with the Missionettes and painting Jesus pictures, she was riding around with a carload of girls, drinking killer cokes and talking about boys.

Daddy didn't normally butt in on our religious training (being backslid himself since his Navy days and smoking cigarettes like a freight train), but he agreed with Momma that Sheena had clever ways and didn't want to be a nurse, so movie shows, carnivals, dance halls, domino halls, swimsuits, devilish-looking pictures in black velvet, makeup, smoking, nail polish, and drinking cokes and riding around in cars were totally off-limits. For all of us girls. It was in the Bible anyhow, he said, but he sure gave Sheena credit for enormous powers of persuasion with her sisters. Daddy's one disagreement with the Bible was short hair. He loved short hair on women and always tried to talk us into cutting our hair even though the Bible clearly said that nothing aggravated God more than looking out into his congregation and seeing long hair on the men and short hair on the girls. Trimming the dead ends was no good neither. Next thing you know, the hair was cut all the way up to their ears and the women were acting like men. It was a step-by-step progression straight to homosexuality. Angels certainly didn't get their hair cut. Momma said what God was really getting at wasn't long hair so much, as *tame* hair, and that the secret was to rinse it in vinegar and rainwater, then wrap the hair—tight—in rubber curlers every Saturday night. Don't matter if your hair is already curly, do it anyhow. Nobody can get enough curly hair. This wasn't pure Bible scripture but Momma's hair was big and bushy and floated over her head and down the middle of her forehead and had given her grief since the day she was born, so she figured she knew hair better than God.

Daddy shouldn't have worried so much about Sheena's influence. It was strong all right, but it was strong *in reverse*. Because her favorite games that she *only* played with Pill and me were Teacher Flunking Ever'body Out and Preacher Sending Ever'body to Hell. Now, why the boys got the Sheena Queen of the Jungle side and we got the teacher and preacher from hell side, I do not know. I just know that you could hear her screaming from a mile out in the pasture in the ramshackle cow shed that we'd turned into a church house with a get-yourself-saved bench fastened from Buttermilk's old rotten feed boards. The pasture was where we conducted our church and Sheena's favorite spot because that was where she could scream the loudest, sending us all to hell or flunking us all out of school, and we could wail in misery and sinfulness without Momma running out and looking to switch our behinds with a peach limb for scaring the daylights out of her because kids screaming meant somebody stepped on a rattlesnake or somebody got pushed out of a tree.

Sheena's specialty was demons with pitchforks and how awful hell will be when the angels start dragging off the sinners in bundles to burn them. My specialty was sliding to my knees faster than a level's bubble in a lopsided house. Oooh, I was cursed with enthusiasm. Sheena's fiercest sinner and her easiest convert. But no! Sheena was very displeased over my easy conversion. Sinners will howl! They won't go willingly. Nooo, they'll weep and wail and gnash their teeth. No water to drink for them for all of eternity. It thrilled Sheena to death! She preached so loud and long on hell's fiery lake that the blood vessels in her neck stuck out like the mustang grapevines that hung in the trees behind the cow shed. If I had had any wits about me I could have swung from the vines and escaped.

Sometimes we tried raising dead animals to life. A pet deer that didn't make it. An alligator's remains after my brothers skinned it and threw it in the yard. Red birds we found on the front porch after they'd rammed into their own reflection in the window. We'd inch our way to a miracle, though. No bigheaded healer going full steam from death to life! No, ma'am. Just inch by inch. Practice practice. First time, we tried praying back a bird's foot that had been gnawed off by a cat. Another time a horny toad's tail that went missing. These looked promising. Do the small miracles first, then the rest should be pretty easy. That was our thinking. When that didn't work, we became loud and elaborate gravediggers, putting gobs of oleander and bougainvillea flowers around the hole and a bunch of chinaberry leaves on top, and when a deer's foot or an alligator's mouth came loose and looked alive to us, we dug the hole again and laid the alligator's mouth or the deer's foot so it wouldn't stick out. Then Sheena said "Dust to dust" three times and I covered the hole.

Momma and Grandma didn't live far from each other; subtract a mile or two of pasture and bayou and it was almost like living at home, which was why it was so easy for Momma to send me and why it was so easy to forget I was there. That's also why I was sitting (hiding) in the potato bin. I was babysitting Grandma after Aunt Teny and her feisty husband and three kids had left her after nine long years. Grandma knew it was about the Fritos but she didn't say so. Grandma didn't argue. Grandma was a Christian and Christians don't fight. She just wanted to know was all.

Actually, I wasn't really babysitting. I didn't know why I was there—which was good because Grandma said she didn't expect nothing from a pilfering kid. She'd seen it all, anyhow. Kids wearing down her fence (walking on it or falling from the chinaberry tree and hitting it going down), kids eating her green peaches, kids eating her Fritos. Kids kids, pilfering kids. That's what happens when the Lord gives you a man. Her lot too. On the firing line for Christ. But Grandma said as long as a kid didn't lie around reading a book, didn't pilfer in her garden or her dresser drawer for doodads, and ate Fritos that *she* gave her, then that kid could stay with her. Well, I liked Fritos and only ate what was given to me and I didn't pilfer much, so I was Momma and Grandma's *fav-o-rite* pick.

Grandma lived in small house and on one wall was a blue swordfish with a sea scene painted on its jagged teeth and against the other wall was a wide blond table with a board underneath that was good for hiding under and occasionally painting Gypsies on with Aunt Teny's red fingernail polish. Staying with Grandma meant two things: shrimp got headed and eggs got picked from her rickety henhouse where snakes and rats lived but weren't shot because after Delbert killed himself Grandma hid the only gun and nobody knew where.

I was the egg getter and my egg-getting method was to throw oyster shells at the henhouse until the chickens ran off, squawking mad, and left their warm eggs to me. Usually my aim was pretty good, but sometimes I hit a chicken and, once, Grandma's best layer, knocking it senseless, and I ran off and hid in the pasture in my older brother's car with the rotten tires and windows rusted shut and the outside mirror smacked off when it was drug out to the pasture two years before—after he'd gone to sleep coming home from a hard ball game and wrecked the thing.

I shouldn't have worried so much about that chicken. Every chicken in the henhouse died at some point under Grandma's foot and only Grandma knew the exact hour. Even her favorites got the foot once they quit laying eggs. The beheading went like this: she placed a short stick on the chicken's neck and held it down with her foot; then she yanked on its legs and the head went one way and the bleeding body went flopping around. Blood everywhere. Then Grandma brought the whole chicken (plus its ripped-off head) into the kitchen and crammed them both into a big pot of boiling water. I was the guard and stationed at the stove with a wooden stick. "Don't let that chicken leave the pot!" Grandma said.

The chicken never fit. Its feet stuck straight up in the air, hard and yellow, peeling and unforgiving. A simmering pot of hot fury. "No matter," Grandma said. "Boil the thing down and make sure it don't float off!" So I did, poking at the chicken until a frothy brown scum looking like week-old ditch water with floating insects spilled over the top of the stove and down around the floor and gummed up my feet.

Everything about a chicken (dead or alive) was good in Grandma's book and worth saving. The eggs! The cotton sack the feed came in! (This was washed, ironed, cut into squares, then made into quilts or dresses.) Chicken necks! White and dark meat! Broth! Gizzards! Feet! Chicken manure! Feathers! Oh oh oh my, especially the feathers. You could stroll outside to Grandma's back porch any day of the week and get smacked in the face by a clothesline of chicken feathers drying in pillowcases. Then at night you could lie down on the biggest prize of all: a mattress cram-packed with feathers.

Grandma was the original Waste Not Want Not-er. It didn't come from the Bible. It came from her. So nothing was so low that it didn't get cooked into something else. Hard, good-for-nothing pears (only the pigs would eat them) were carved and parboiled and made into pies that tasted like apple (it was the dash of cinnamon, she said). Mulberries that rotted on the trees or were so useless that they were trodden underfoot were made into purple pies. Unripened green grapes from the mustang grape-vines roping through the oak trees were made into green pies, and if her green-grape pie happened to set our little teeth on edge, well, Grandma reminded us of the story of the neighborhood lady who raised all her babies on bread sopped in bean juice and how we ought to be thankful for that green-grape pie and not complain lest the devil come into her kitchen.

Nothing was thrown out. Not food scraps. Not dirty wash water in a bucket. Not jelly jars, mason jars, lids, pieces of cardboard, Christmas cards, greeting cards, bread wrappers, strings from bread wrappers. Once Grandma made the local news for having the biggest ball of string in the county and a picture was taken of her sitting in a rocking chair with her spun-glass hair tied up in a ponytail and over that a hair net and over that a pink curler cap to ward off pneumonia. (Grandma also self-doctored. Red monkey blood for her ears and fingers and toes and cotton balls for every hole in her body to ward off cold air, poisons, and infections of all kind. Grandma didn't believe in doctors.) But that ball of string didn't sit around going to waste! Nosiree. She crocheted two dozen string rugs out of that giant ball and when that ran out, she ripped old clothes neighbor ladies (less thrifty neighbor ladies) had given her into strips and wove those into rag rugs. Then Grandma sat in her old rocker in her old place and the heels of the sewing machine rubbed the floor raw with her ingenuity.

So if Grandma had known I was hiding in an empty potato bin and not making myself useful, she'd have said, "Land a'Goshen, child! Ain't you got nothing better to do? That's the terriblest thing I've ever seen!" Then, straight out, she'd have asked Sister Jackson to come and pray the laziness devil out of me 'cause Sister Jackson could pray you right out of your socks. Grandma could pray, too, but she didn't trust her prayers on important family matters, saying if you're asking Jesus for a Rolls-Royce but you only got bicycle faith, guess what you'll get? A bicycle!

Well, it really wasn't a bicycle Grandma got. Grandma got dead Delbert. But that was years and years ago. Before I was born. Before the Fritos. During the *terrible times.* When she and her preaching husband and a carload of kids first arrived in Texas and searched every back road and mud-infested bayou for just the right church to shower the Holy Ghost on them. They found it in an old Pentecostal church beside a chinaberry tree that kids climbed and hung swings on and halfway around the trunk for no good reason was an old shirt tied up and rotten. In spite of all that searching, though, Delbert, their fifteen-year-old, unsaved son, was lost to Lucifer and his legions.

First Delbert slipped toward the tattoo parlor and got himself a big red heart tattooed on his chest. Then he definitely faltered when two months to the day after he got his first gun and showed it off in the front yard in a short jacket and boots, with the gun dangling from his hand, Delbert shot himself as he was climbing into a boat and got himself a hole to match a snake-eyed domino. On his brand-new tattoo.

Grandma knew the situation. She wasn't fooling herself. Delbert had been drug from the boat to the house and the bullet went clear out his back so he'd been dead awhile. Then she quit thinking with her head. That's the first rule of raising the dead: hardheaded saints need to be crucified in their skulls and soaked with the Holy Spirit! So Grandma let Jesus, who was sitting right there on the armchair, tell her what to do next. "Forget that gun, Rosa Belle," Jesus said. "Read John, chapter fourteen, verse twelve!"

Grandma asked Jesus to please forgive her for forgetting the words to that scripture in all the gun commotion.

She knew there were three raisings of the dead in the Old Testament and three raisings in the New Testament and Jesus raised the dead along with Peter, Paul, Elijah, and Elisha. But please, Jesus, just let her get her Bible out. So Jesus did and she got her Bible out and thumbed over to the book of John and read:

"Verily, verily, I say unto you, He that believeth on me, the works that I do shall he do also; and greater works than these shall he do; because I go unto my Father."

Jesus said, "Just grab ahold of your faith, Rosa Belle. HOLD ON HOLD ON. No matter what Lucifer says or does, just believe with all your heart that life will overcome death this very hour."

Grandma knew everything Jesus said was true. And the Bible don't lie. Regular folks can't do nothing on their own, but they can if they believe Jesus is working behind the scenes. Miracles weren't hard. Everybody knew that miracles came straight from heaven and there was probably a whole warehouse up there with little slots holding the different miracles. Here's a miracle to straighten out your legs. And there's a miracle to make that eye see. Why, there's Delbert's miracle lying right there in that slot. It was the *belief* in miracles that was hard 'cause that came from us, natural-born sinners all the way from Eve who was the Mother of All Sinners. So if somebody doubted a miracle, a split second later she just made God a liar and God didn't like being called a liar. That would rain down hate and strife.

Grandma said she had heard stories all her Christian life of how a sister or a brother had been anointed by the

Holy Ghost and laid hands on a cold stilled body—some dead for ten hours!—and rose it up from the dead. She'd heard shouting testimonies of how a brother had levitated in prayer, floated up and left his shoes behind. She had seen anointed men and women in their little church in Oklahoma look eyeball-to-eyeball at poisonous snakes and no harm had come to them. Because they believed. She just couldn't let the devil distract her with his lies.

So Grandma shoved the creeping mass of hysterical girls out of the kitchen where Delbert was laid out on the table and she wedged a chair against the doorknob and waited on Jesus to work behind the scenes. Jesus told her to pray for life, even though death was tempting her to doubt it could take place. The cold hands and face. The blue-tinged lips and fingertips. The gaping bloody hole. Those symptoms . . . the presence of death . . . were the devil's lies. God *always* responded to prayer. And if he didn't, who's fault was that? Not God's. Look for it elsewhere, Rosa Belle.

Grandma said she looked hell in the eye that day. Oh, the misery and suffering she saw as she tried to pull Delbert back from the clutches of hell. It was so hot in that kitchen that there was a vaporlike stream everywhere and the flames would lap up and fork over her feet. Later when she looked at her shoes, the soles had fire marks where the flames had licked the rubber.

Five hours later Delbert was dead and Grandma was very much alive. Grandma's excuse was Delbert was a bit more dead than she expected and she got in too big a hurry. You can't rush the Lord on deliverance 'cause the Lord don't wait on you. It's you that waits upon the Lord. So

Grandma washed Delbert's chest and face and hands and sat in her old rocker in her old place beneath the sawed-off teeth of a swordfish hanging on the wall and read her Bible until Grandpa came home. Then the family buried Delbert in his Sunday best and Grandma shoved his gun where nobody could find it. She couldn't do nothing about that tattoo. He was just buried with it.

A year later Grandpa was outside in a field and tying a mule to a plow when a lightning storm came and the Angel of Death took the mule and all the coins melted in Grandpa's pocket. Grandma said her failed effort with Delbert plus a lightning-struck husband all in the same year was a sign from God sayin', "You got bicycle faith, Rosa Belle."

Well, maybe so. But she was devout as the dickens to a radio evangelist from San Antonio that she gave all her hard-earned shrimp-heading money to and she was ready to die at a moment's notice with her funeral outfit in the bottom drawer. Death was the last enemy. Just read 1 Corinthians 15:26. Next to heaven, dying was the next best thing. So when I walked with her to the cemetery to help pull weeds around Grandpa and Delbert's graves but instead hung out on the barbwire fence and hollered about ghosts sitting on the tombstones, Grandma had no sympathy. She bent straight from the waist with her knees locked like a thirteen-year-old girl's and went to town on the sticker burrs and the ceda beans. "Fiddlesticks, child," she said. "There's nothing to fear in a graveyard. You will understand in time. Just give it some time, child. You'll want to die too."

THREE

Grandma ate Fritos in a glass of buttermilk for dinner and supper and that plus giving the radio evangelist all her shrimp-heading money was driving two of her daughters batty and two not so much. Momma was the oldest and said (actually, she said this a lot), "Let it all fall in the ocean! See who cares!" Aunt Silver was next oldest and she was privately pleased because she was a Pentecostal youth minister and evangelized in cold cold Idaho with her pastor husband when they weren't trying to get back to warm Texas, and she knew the whereabouts of God, Jesus, and the Holy Ghost's mind on most religious matters because she asked them point-blank. And they answered point-blank. They told her Grandma was on the warpath for God, going all the way with Christ, and for that Grandma could expect three reactions from her less holy daughters: 1) she would be rejected; 2) she would be cast out; 3) she would be stoned.

Aunt Teny and Aunt June Bug were the two young-est daughters—both Baptist, both lipstick wearers, both gold-hoop-earring wearers—but after marrying and leaving home, they both went as far as they could in opposite directions. Aunt June Bug went south to the rolling Gulf beaches where you could visit her if you crossed the bay on a ferryboat, went down a streetful of sand dunes, climbed steps onto a stilted house, and didn't mind a trio of flea-bitten greyhound dogs sleeping underneath you at night.

Aunt Teny went west to Houston, then east to Grandma's bayou house, then across town to a house that was opposite a gas filling station where her kids bought a zillion Dr Peppers and drank every one with a warm mayonnaise sandwich.

Neither one was fixing to stone Grandma. But they were hot as tar about the evangelist taking all her money. "You'd think a year's worth of shrimp-heading checks from an old widow woman would be plenty for that snake-oil salesman. Man of God, my hind foot! That man oughta be locked up!"

Grandma just snorted back at them, "Oooh, child, don't let the Lord hear you say that! What if he told you one of your legs was plenty? How'd you like that? One leg! Prissing around on one leg!"

Then the girls found a newspaper story about the evangelist caught in a hotel room in San Antonio with a stripper and they cut it out and left it on Grandma's sewing table, thinking it might burst her little bubble on that radio man, but the news clipping didn't do none of that. Grandma said she didn't believe in worldly besotted newspapers! That was more of Satan's handiwork. Then she called Aunt Teny and Aunt June Bug Satan's henchmen, which was almost the same thing the evangelist told his Radio Land listeners— that he was under attack by the devil's henchmen and his sin in that hotel room just showed the awful power those devils possessed but with prayers and donations coming in, and Jesus willing, he'd make it out alive.

It wasn't exactly hind-end backward, but it wasn't close to what my aunts' original intent was when they cut out the newspaper clipping, so they gave up on giving Grandma THE FACTS. She wasn't listening to nobody anyhow and if their sister Silver made it back from Idaho, there'd be double the dose of hard-necked, hardheaded religiosity. Heck, Grandma might even give the entire house to the evangelist. Send him the last nails in the floor!

So there was the second reason I was staying with Grandma, other than that first one I didn't understand. Aunt Teny said she had given me my first birthday whooping and sewed ever' dress I'd ever worn and I had lived in her house in Houston until I was nearly three months old, so I was her accomplice for life. My mission that summer was to hide the Fritos and tell her or June ever' time Grandma mailed out a shrimp check.

Can a kid hide Fritos from a seventy-year-old grandma? Was that legal? Can folks pilfer letters from the United States Post Office? Well, I didn't know. But I was nine years old and did pretty well ever' cotton-picking thing I was told, so I was walking to the bay with Grandma to take names and jot notes. I had a job.

Grandma's idea of a job was shrimp heading or dewberry picking or cotton picking or egg getting. Take your pick. It didn't matter to her. Being particular was all about vanity anyhow and vanity was the devil. So there. Only thing that mattered to Grandma was sending ever' red cent she made to the radio evangelist who was trying to raise up Christ Consciousness in the Dead Continent of America where lust, greed, and sin wrestled, uncontrolled, for the souls of Americans. Sickness and cancer were rampant. Dirt and filth had taken over America's cities! It was Calcutta without the cows, and humdrum love offerings wasn't cuttin' that type of problem. God would spew that lukewarm love offering out of his mouth. So even with the demons hanging off his coattails and vying for his soul, the evangelist was confident that Jesus would move hearts and provide the cash to keep his radio station open. Yes yes. Jesus would provide. Why, just recently this sister listening in Ohio sent in a fabulous story telling how her car's motor was healed on the highway coming to church. God wasn't leaving her stranded! Another wonderful testimony from Florida told how Jesus had made a listener's parrot speak in an unknown chirp, praising God. Why, there were reports by the hundreds. Fantastic encounters with Jesus Christ and the Holy Spirit. Because when you're living close to God, personal messages from God are routine. Healings of all kinds—corrected spinal injuries, lengthened legs, fingers growing back, one dollar bill turning into ten, broken washing machines working again. So grandmas and grandpas out there in Radio Listening Land. In Jesus's precious name! JESUS-uh! Grandmas and grandpas, turn on your radio and listen!

So Grandma scribbled out a shaky little shrimping check and I turned on her pink radio with the station permanently marked with nursing tape to seal the preaching channel for good, just like the nursing tape and the little bottle of red monkey blood (Mercurochrome) sealed shrimp poisoning from Grandma's fingers for good. Then in the winter when Grandma's front door and all her windows were shut and the intensity of the gas heater and the yelling on that religious channel could blow you away, Grandma just stuffed cotton balls in her ears (the edges doctored with red monkey blood) and said the hollering didn't bother her. It was just heaven hollering.

So heaven hollered in the spring, summer, winter, and fall. It was round-the-clock radio evangelism! Sometimes, though, three heaping mountains of oyster shells stinkin' to the high heaven in Grandma's front yard blocked the radio reception. It was unintentional though. The oyster shells didn't mean to. Not devil inspired. They had been sitting for years, first ripped howling from their mother reef in the bay by ugly rusting barges, then dumped unceremoniously onto county trucks that hauled them to Grandma's front yard to later pave every road in town. But in the in-between time of Grandma's front yard and a county road, winter-starved kids like us scooted down the oyster mountain on the wrenched-off hoods of wrecked trucks and sometimes our own tail ends, which was why we all ended up with scars we will carry to our grave. Didn't matter. Didn't matter. Jesus healed every cut and trans-formed the hard static into heavenly waves and Grandma heard anyhow. Minor miracles right there.

Right after Grandma's radio program was turned off until the same time tomorrow, me and Grandma lit out for the fish house. I was wearing a blue squaw dress that Aunt Teny made from a pattern cut from a grocery sack and carrying a scar to my grave, and Grandma was wearing her ever'day blue dress that smelled like the cedar chest she kept her good blankets in and carrying a paper sack with Fritos, two plastic aprons, baby powder, a tiny bottle that looked like tooth-ache medicine but was really red monkey blood to ward off shrimp poison, a new pair of pink Playtex gloves still in their box for me, and an older, stinkier pair of gloves with the fingers cut off and wrapped in a bread wrapper for her.

Grandma said, "Pick up your pace, child, and pass me that umbrella." So I picked up my pace and passed her the umbrella. We needed that umbrella; it was hot in the road and a long walk too, and little oyster-dust tornadoes puffed up and died around every bare toe. I didn't wear shoes. Shoes were a big waste of time at the fish house. There were a hundred delicious things you could stick your toes in. Grandma was more practical. Grandma was wearing heavy-duty shoes with heavy-duty stockings that made her legs look they were covered in poison oak (they weren't), and she walked down the middle of the road like she owned it. And no scooting off. Scooting off would land her in the oyster dust piled as high as my head on the side of the road. Well, it wasn't actually as high as my head (Grandma would call that a lie), but it was higher than the middle of the road where she walked and trucks drove, knocking oyster dust hither and thither into the ditches, onto the barbwire fences, and covering every tree and vine for half a mile in every direction. Mainly, though, no trucks came because their time was over with; they'd vamoosed since before dawn when the shrimpers left on their boats and left truck keys dangling in warm trucks. The trucks wouldn't hit the road again until later that night.

But once or twice a car stopped and a lady (it was always a lady in no hurry) would lean out the window and say, Howdee, Missus Mullins, and Grandma would say howdee back and the lady would say, How you feelin', Missus

Mullins? And Grandma would wiggle her ten fingers at her and keep walking. Wiggling fingers was the extent of Grandma's joking. That was the extent of her conversation, too, because work was where we were headed and it wasn't no picnic.

I had no favorite job, but if I did, it certainly wasn't cleaning Sister Pearl's house or picking cotton, which I volunteered for once, dragging a sack through the dirt for half a day and ten nickels. That was my last time there.

The worst job, though, was shrimp heading. Shrimp heading sounded fun but it wasn't. Two Mexican fish-house hands threw tubs of smelly shrimp onto a metal table and women in plastic aprons and rubber gloves pinched the shrimp heads off, stuck the heads in a bucket, weighed the bucket, got a number, and at the end of the day made what all those numbers added up to. Some women pinched heads with two hands and got a high number but a few (the slooow headers) pinched with one hand and got almost zero. I was a one-hander, an elbow leaner, and almost a nuisance in the fish house. If I had one dream at that table it was that the next tub of shrimp was BIG shrimp with heads like gophers' and every one weighing a ton. There wasn't nothing I hated worse than little shrimp with heads that weighed like chicken feathers. Grandma knew this too and always drew a line through the shrimp in front of me with her rubber glove, saying, "Now, don't be such a greedy gut, child! Do them little ones first!" So the squashed heads went into my bucket and the rest of the shrimp went to the fish house owner. It was almost like picking cotton. Same kinda price, anyhow. Two cents a pound.

Grandma was the fastest header and the fish house owner's sister was second. There was no race, no keeping score, but everybody knew who was the fastest. Even the fish house owner knew and ever' time Grandma walked to the scales with yet another bucket of shrimp heads and the Mexican guy took her bucket and hung it on the scales and subtracted the bucket weight, then put the leftover number down in a little spiral notebook tied with a string to a nail, the fish house owner touched his hat. (Grandma was a fine Christian woman and didn't lock her doors at night, but she kept a separate tally on a piece of paper in her pocketbook. She didn't trust Mexican guys.)

There were two rules at the dock. First rule: the men don't talk to the women and the women don't talk to the men. They can pretend that they might but they're just being polite. Second rule: Just be polite. So when the fish house owner came in and looked at all the women headers who had arrived and saw that they already had on their aprons and gloves and were standing ready on their spot at the heading table and he said, Howdee, ladies, they all smiled back and said nothing, not even the fish house owner's sister who headed shrimp just like us. (The brother and sister didn't talk except in the evening when they argued over the fish house they both owned but he ran.)

In the beginning the shrimp were iced down and firm and squeezing their heads off didn't obliterate them totally. And there were enough BIG shrimp scattered in the heap to make things interesting, but then the day wore on and the table got warm and the shrimp got little

(I wasn't the only one going after the big shrimp first!) and went to mush and that's when the women started talking; there was no rule at the docks about women talking with other women. While Grandma normally preferred SILENCE IS GOLDEN or something like that, she had not a shred of embarrassment about asking folks if they were washed in the blood of the Lamb. Were they saved and going to heaven? After all, Grandma said, she wasn't the one in charge of her life. The Holy Ghost was the one in charge. And of all the heavenly hosts, he had the easiest hurt feelings, so if the Holy Ghost wanted Grandma to ask the young girl standing next to her if she knew the Lord, then Grandma better ask. So Grandma said, Dearie, do you know Jesus as your personal savior? And the girl said, Yes, ma'am, she was baptized in the Baptist Church when she was twelve. Well, Grandma knew all about the Baptist Church and how backsliding into sin wasn't in their dictionary, but that ignorance wasn't gonna keep them from sliding into hell. No, ma'am. She might just be an ordinary radio listener and not have set foot inside a church door since the day that deacon laughed at her when she fell into a ditch and couldn't get herself out, but she had iron britches when it came to Bible scripture.

Just throw something at her and see if she couldn't cite scripture and verse back. She also knew loads and loads about children standing on their feet all day long and heading shrimp with their grandmas. Backbreaking work, but Christian children don't complain. There were a half-dozen scriptures pertaining to just that one quality. NO COMPLAINING.

Well, I didn't complain but I had a dozen reasons for leaving the heading table. Finger pricks I had to examine under the bright sunlight on the docks. Torn gloves and aprons that needed retaping out on the docks. Washing my feet under the water faucet out on the docks because I had failed to wear shoes again and shrimp juice had glued me to the fish house floor. All my excuses eventually led me to the same place at the docks, either lying over a hole in the wharf and watching crabs fight the hardheads over the shrimp heads thrown out by the fish house boys or sitting under the wharf on broken bits of concrete and oyster shells with my feet in the water and watching dead crabs float by, harmless, their feelers and dried backs high out of the water like a can of dried-up sardines. Sometimes hardheads fat as gophers would cruise by my toes and dart like flies when I wiggled my foot. But my idleness was always short-lived. Idleness was the devil's workshop and Grandma's eye was never far. "Quick quick, child. More tubs of shrimp!"

So we headed more tubs of shrimp. Then more, then more. I was bored out of my skull and leaned on my elbows against the heading table and contemplated the slimy metal table. There was nothing alive, just butchered shrimp under my gloves. No head left. Nothing to weigh. No two pennies. I grabbed a chunk of ice and washed my face.

Finally the Mexican fish house guys wore out or else we headed ever' tub of shrimp in that ice vault. I suspect it was the shrimp giving out because our fish house guys weren't paid to be lazy. Then the women at the table slumped like old party balloons. *PSPHHhhhhhhhh*. They slowly untied their aprons, took off their rubber gloves, and then hosed the shrimp slime off every rubber remnant they had capable of a shrimp smell. It was only after the aprons and gloves were laid out on the wharf or against a piling to air out that the women finally opened their paper-sack dinners.

The docks were part wood and part cement, with gobs of oyster shells thrown underneath to keep the lapping water from hauling off the fish house, and in the in-and-out process (high tide, low tide, moon rising, moon falling) scraps of garbage loosened like bad tooth fillings—and catfish the size of railway boxcars, which I was told could swallow a child whole, gobbled down every morsel. Rotten shrimp. Decayed fish heads. Drowned cats. Half-eaten sandwiches. No wonder I never ate catfish!

Anyhow, there was no running on the docks, just serious serious Mexicans pulling tubs of shrimp and ice back and forth when there was tubs to be pulled and pulling nothing when nothing was going on. And nothing was going on. It was hot. The heat squiggled off the water. It was Frito time for Grandma and me. She handed me a handful and I ate my Fritos, one by one, and watched my hands turn orange. An occasional shrimp head bobbed on the water and the sun turned it orange too.

If I was a real lucky kid that day and hadn't hogged the big shrimp particularly bad and Grandma wasn't on her sodie-water tangent. (Usually she was because foolishness was not lost on Grandma. She knew loads about tin-can bums and cigarette sots and how they squandered God's money on cigarettes and sodie water and chewing gum and tattoos.) I got to walk down the road to the sportsman's bait shop and buy a red sodie water to wash down the Fritos.

The bait lady was the aunt of the fish house owners where we headed shrimp, and she sat behind her counter and watched her customers with fifty-year-old eyes. She wore light-colored pants, a white shirt, white tennis shoes, and a cap on her head that was identical to and said the same thing as the dozen others strung on a fishing line across the front of her shop. All were sun rotted and FOR SALE. Grandma said the bait lady had money but you couldn't tell it by looking at her bait shop. When was the last time a mop was run through that place?

After my sodie water, I gave up. I was tired. Tired of the standing, tired of the relentless pinch pinch pinch, tired of the fishy smells in every corner of the fish house and on the road and behind the trucks and under the docks and on my hands and feet. But not Grandma. She didn't recognize defeat. She was helping feed the souls in corrupt America. Oh no, not yet not yet, minions of Satan! So it was back to the fish house to wait for more boats to bring in more tubs of shrimp. Lordy Lordy.

Evening at a fish house isn't because the sun goes down. It's because the boats come in. Same as sunrise: it's because the boats leave. Boats are the Mecca the fishermen go to every morning, and they leave before daybreak. I heard them in my sleep: the engines starting up, first one, then two, then the whole fleet until the dock was empty and what a sad pitiful sight. All her fishermen gone. Then the boats returned and the whole thing went in reverse. But in the in-between time of a harbor empty and one returned to life, the bay was a hot gray smear with nothing to differen-

tiate the east side from the west side except a sunny after-
noon that stretched on and on—full of shadows on water
and shadows playing games and looking like a woman's
body one minute, then the next minute a little kid holding
a deck bucket. I was sitting on an overturned shrimp tub
outside the fish house and seeing a kid riding a donkey and
holding a stick when a shrimp boat plowed in and messed
up the whole thing.

There's a saying that the good die young, but in this
case, that wasn't quite true. The shrimp captain pulling the
disabled boat that messed up my mirage said Sambo had
it coming. But that wasn't the first thing he said. The first
thing he said was, "Get my got-dang rope!"

Then it got confusing as heck because suddenly ever'body
went running around on the docks that nobody runs
around on and somebody yelled, "Take it around yonder!"
But nobody did. Then somebody else hollered, "Stay back
stay back. My God, stay back!"

I was doctoring the situation with my own truth juice,
because nobody was paying us women headers a drop of
attention. We were whisked back into the fish house like
we were a bunch of light-skinned babies on a hot day and
told, Stay away, ma'am. Don't look, ma'am. Oh my gosh,
oh my lord. Then all the men went down to the docks and
hung around a bloody tarp.

That's when we heard "Sambo had it coming." It was
pretty loud. Ever' woman in the fish house heard it.
Somebody agreed, then somebody else said, "The damage
is done. Leave it alone."

Finally one of the Mexicans wandered over to the boat

and took a good look under the tarp that nobody was touching except with their rubber boots ever' now and then. Then he walked back to the fish house and said to nobody at all, "Señor Sambo got a gun kinda mess."

Eventually we figured it out without a single man, other than the Mexican, running up to tell us. One shrimper got shot dead and one shrimper went missing, and the shrimper missing was my daddy's baby brother, Archie Don, and probably shot dead too, because why would one shrimper be shot dead and not two? Didn't make sense.

Someone made a suggestion. Call the game wardens. Nope. Nope. Hell, nope! Better dead than calling the game wardens. Call the constable! Or call the sheriff! Some shrimpers agreed, but some said less enemies among the shrimpers meant less things to explain. Less less. That type of thing.

Then Sambo was wrapped tight in his bloody tarp (the Mexican was right) and hauled off the shrimp boat to a truck bed that the fish house owner got from somebody because it sure wasn't his; his truck bed was already loaded down with shrimp. Sambo's body was headed for the funeral house. But maybe not, maybe not. A car shot to the fish house door, ground to a halt, and threw oyster dust ever'where. A woman with short hair and a cotton dress pulled tight around her brown knees jumped out and ran over to Sambo and shouted in his dead ear, "I hope you puked your guts out first!"

The Mexican said, "Ees Señor Sambo's wiiife."

FOUR

Lost, unsaved boys did it ever' time for Grandma.
And even though Archie Don was not lost (just
dead) and not a boy (he was over forty) he definitely hit
the jackpot on unsaved—he had two wives and divorced
both—so Grandma did her charitable Christian best by
loaning me out to Daddy's side of the fence. To Chief, my
daddy's daddy. Chief would sooner take a blunt end of an
ax to his head then go to church or associate with any of the
practitioners of such (including religious radio programs),
but he was ready to check out the rat-trap trailer his son
Archie Don, and sometimes Sambo, lived in because the
shrimpers were acting like Archie's missing fishing pole
and a missing rifle were the last things on earth to puzzle
over. Chief knew different. So when Grandma told me
to go climb in the truck with Chief because he was too
decrepit to be driving around by himself and was liable to
kill himself, Chief let her have her way.

Arch's truck was parked at the docks with the keys
dangling just like every shrimper's truck. Normally old
rusted trucks that sit at the bay all day long are notorious
fussy starters. Their gears are worn out. Parts are missing or borrowed (stolen). And they want lots of coaxing
and pleading and threats that their worthless rusty hides
are gonna be run off into the bayou. But Arch's truck
was small potatoes; it just wanted a little grinding and
some gas pumping and then it was up and running and

Chief took off like he might roll the ol' speedometer up to twenty.

The truck was flat cleaned out of paper wads and last month's bills but cigarette butts were fighting with the oyster dust for attention. Oyster dust covered every-thing—even the vinyl covering on the seats. It looked like a momma had gone nutty with the baby powder 'cause oyster dust looks like nothing if not fine baby powder. But actually the dust had paid Arch's truck a little visit through the rusted hole in the floorboard, just like the dust had a key and let itself in. The mirror dangling outside the truck was rusted to pieces. So was the fender. Once when Archie was hauling a shrimp net to the bay, down that same fender hole went the net and it wrapped itself twice around the wheel and lifted the truck clean into the air. I forget how Arch got out of that mess.

Chief was part Cherokee or Blackfoot (he never said which) and talked minor talk to dead folks. (That was his talent, same as mine was imagining myself on the moon when I wasn't.) So after he drove a quarter mile down the road and pulled into a bone-bare yard full of run-down trailers and half-done skiffs sitting on barrels, Chief walked into the front door of Arch's trailer like he was a human Geiger counter fixing to measure radiation in a land mine. Two feet, four feet. Nothing, just mild humming. Beep beep beeping. Then he walked some more, talked aloud some more; then he stopped in Archie's room where the iron bed was unmade and sunk in the middle. The window was half-raised. Chief turned and look at me and his eyebrows went up and hung there for a minute. BEEEP.

Neither of us said a word. One face turned to another face, two dark things, a little one and a big one. I had no idea what the dead said to Chief. I didn't even talk with the living.

Then Chief turned and walked to the kitchen where a black skillet crusted over with day-old cooked cabbage looked like it had been used as a football by someone and kicked clean across the room. A drawer near the sink was yanked out and on the floor. Knives and forks everywhere. Chief reached down and picked up a knife and acted like he didn't know exactly what he was going to do with the thing. It was just a piece of metal lying against his leg while he walked. Might be a cane. There was a cracked mirror on the bathroom wall and Chief leaned in, checked his teeth, and then pulled the knife up, grabbed his hair, and cut a chunk. When that handful was cut, he dropped it and grabbed another.

Chief came out of the bathroom. His red plaid shirt was loose at the shoulders where he'd lost all that weight after a stingray got him last winter and the hair on the right side of his head was shorter than the hair on the left. I said, "Heck a mile, Chief. What'd you go do that for?"

ONE summer when I was six I smuggled cold mayonnaise sandwiches and sweet homemade pickles from the kitchen, cut a skiff's rotten towline, stole the skiff, then frantically bailed water from the old rotten thing with my tennis shoes. I was headed for the reefs and the herons and the random pilings sticking out of the water. Really, I didn't know where I was headed. Timbuktu or Alakazam. Maybe Black Jack Island where Chief was raised. Someplace more entertaining than Grandma's hard-packed chicken yard overgrown with mesquite trees and ceda beans.

The whole time I was bailing water, I was more on the sinking side than the floating side and my feet wrinkled like the sand when the tide leaves. But at least I was in the skiff and not in the water, and a good thing too, because I couldn't swim a lick. Even a bathtub (and especially hot water in a bathtub, and don't ask me why hot water did it worse than cold water) was a scary situation.

Chief didn't swim, neither. Not a drop, he said, and it was because he never had the leisure time to play around in the water when he was a kid. But the real reason was his killer daddy. Chief said give him a nickel for every story he'd heard about a fisherman's mean-tempered daddy and he would be a rich fisherman. But his daddy really was the honest-to-God cross-your-heart-and-hope-to-die killer daddy.

Chief's killer dad was an Arkansas Indian so Chief was part Arkansas Indian, but his baby brother was a full-blooded sand dune on Black Jack Island. The baby brother wasn't born a sand dune but became one at age two when he plus six more rode to Texas on a wagon from Arkansas, where the family was then drug out on a skiff to the forlorn Black Jack Peninsula by their killer dad, who next tried drowning Chief by throwing him over the homemade skiff, sayin', Sink or swim, boy. Make up your mind.

Chief's daddy kept a lot of information to himself so he was probably already figuring out the knotholes and the potholes of leaving an island he'd just arrived on and a family he'd had for some time and probably thought that a pitch over the skiff would either drown Chief outright, making the burden lighter, or make Chief stronger, meaner, tougher, leaner—in other words, able to catch more fish to support the family he was fixing to leave.

Well, hell, somebody had to! Wasn't gonna be him. After all, he came from Arkansas, land of the hot-springs water, and he was in a bad situation on this hot island. He was a man hankering for relief from a fever but all he was getting was more mosquito bites on top of his malaria. It was survival he had in mind.

So he left one night never to return, saying he was headed in for supplies and so long and adios. Soon after the momma went depressed and the kids went wild as kids left unattended in a howling south wind straight off the Gulf will do. The kids hauled every stick of driftwood they could find up on their end of the beach and built a giant bonfire. Chief's baby brother was two at the time and followed Chief ever'where, toddling around on his fat sunburned legs, and that night he followed Chief out to the fire and fell in.

In a roundabout way, the kids blamed the wind and not the daddy for the baby dying because at least the wind was there to blame. Outta sight, outta mind. So it was the wind's fault. Then the daddyless family buried the baby in the one spot they thought the howling wind couldn't possibly reach: the valley between two sand dunes. But the south wind found the baby and blew hot sand until the baby became just another dune on the gulf beach.

Chief's momma never said if it was the wind's fault that the daddy left and the baby died. She just never said. Then one day she took what was left of her kids (not the dead baby) and left in a hailstorm on a wagon she later sold for their rail tickets back to Arkansas. Chief wouldn't leave. He stayed on, half starved, half sun-struck, half loco from trying to uncover what the howling wind was so busy burying. Lack of food made him finally quit digging, but it was the wind that made him get up and move. She hollered over and over, You're gonna be another sand dune you're gonna be another sand dune you're gonna be another sand dune.

Chief eventually wandered upon another family living in a tent on the beach. That tent family had a French-born momma who spoke no English and smoked a smelly dark pipe in the evening while she sewed cast nets that took days to make and brought in little besides the shrimp it caught in its fine meshes, which the momma later sun-dried on the roof of the tent for supper at night. Luckily, too, that daddy was sane as a one-dollar bill. But life is a fickle friend that likes to make fools and liars of us all, so the wind that made his brother a sand dune now carried Chief out every morning to fish, and in the evening when his skiff was full, she carried him back in. And on the days she didn't, Chief poled himself in.

Grandpa did become a leaner, tougher fisherman and he sold his fish to an old man at an oyster house who was tougher than him. (The old man wouldn't let him use a shovel—only handpicked fish—because he said he wasn't paying no two cents a pound for fish slime.) Then when fishing got bad (and fishing always always goes bad) Chief went to living with a crew of men on the Guadalupe River who were babysitting a homemade still. Chief's job was to

sit in a tree with a big buffalo rifle and wait on the somebodies who might come to bust them up and when they
showed up brace himself for a fall, 'cause that's what the
rifle would make him do when he pulled the trigger.

Four months later that all changed when a woman who
had been hired to teach seven grades for thirty dollars a
month in a one-room schoolhouse came down the river
with another party. Normally the moonshiners' plan in
operation was to force boats off the river, get them to taste
the brew, and make them accessories to the brew making.
Well, this woman was a devout Baptist and a schoolteacher
and right off she said she would have none of that sin. Then
she spotted Chief sitting high in a river oak with his buffalo
rifle and demanded to know why he wasn't in school. Well,
Chief had no good reason so the woman inducted him to
school on the spot.

Chief never offered any extras on that story. No fillers.
Nothing to soften the blows except to say that as far as Little
Brother Sand Dune was concerned, he could go out there
any day of the week and talk to that sand dune and that sand
dune would talk baby talk right back at him. Other than that,
he wouldn't say what kind of Indian he or Little Brother
Sand Dune were, saying real daddies and fake daddies and
killer daddies were all the same to him. If he had a choice,
though, he would pick the Karankawa Indians that roamed
the Texas beaches and ate sun-dried shrimp and sometimes
a human leg. Definitely not the Arkansas Indians.

Chief would sit in his favorite chair, telling stories full
of shark teeth and fish hooks hitting bone and hail- and

windstorms coming outta nowhere to sink stupid unsus-
pecting boats with their stupid captains. Chief said don't
mess with the wind and she ain't bad. No more than a
woman wanting to play nice after a knife attack was bad.
Then he'd laugh and point his empty pipe at us kids and
we'd grab it, fighting and scratching and hitting everybody else to get it. The winner got to poke his pipe full of
sweet damp dark tobacco and sometimes too was handed
the Jergens lotion he always kept close by to rub down his
sore leg that was hooked by a giant stingray. Then when
Chief thought we were least ready and most unsuspect-
ing (the one trait he picked up from his killer daddy) he'd
shove his big dirty feet in our faces and yell, "It's Blackfoot,
you pack of heathens!"

FIVE

urder in a fishing town is like the day before a hurricane hits. Everybody knows it's gonna be a terrible tragedy but they can't help feeling excited. Grandma didn't feel an ounce of the stuff. She said she'd seen enough trifling, measly weighted, unsaved men in her lifetime to know that when bad things happened it was God's retribution. Getting run over by boats, hands mangled in towing cables, and head-on car collisions where body parts got strewn all over the road were all part of God's judgment, and she had not the slightest doubt that Sambo (and Archie Don too) was cut down directly by the judgment hand of God. It was just a little foretaste of what was fixing to come during the Terrible Tribulation. And if any one of my cousins dared smirk during one of her finger waggings on the Great and Terrible Tribulation, Grandma said, "It's amusing to you now, child, but it won't be so funny when you drop into the fiery furnace of hell." Christian living wasn't a bit funny to Grandma even though her motto (cross-stitched and hanging over the door) was NEVER BE SORROWFUL AND WORRYING, BUT ALWAYS REJOICING. It was very confusing.

Murderwise, it was slooow progress. The sheriff hadn't been alerted yet, but that was normal. Sambo and Archie Don were fishermen so it was fishermen's business and fishermen took care of their own kind in their own way and on their own time. So while day and night alternated like it mattered, it didn't really. The shrimpers went out on the bay, but they worried like old women sitting at home on the front porch with a cat in their lap. Even the normal fish, shrimp, and oyster smells started to smell different. Two-day-old gun smoke was what they smelled like. So the fishermen got in a quiet circle with their legs hitched on somebody's truck bumper, and they talked. Should we post a harbor cop? Who's got the money for that? You got the money for that? Nope, hell nope. Well, who's gonna watch for that dang game warden—'cause if we don't, ain't it us courting disaster next?

It was a heavy-duty question for a small town whose own mayor openly flaunted his illegal nets and even once after a game warden confiscated the said illegal nets and then went home to get a little shut-eye, had the audacity to sneak down to the game warden's skiff and steal them back. In the end, though, they did nothing. Fishermen are notorious for that. Doing something on land looked and felt too much like . . . like farming! And they weren't farmers, they were fishermen! So it took two full days for the sheriff to find out about the murder from the embalmer's snot-nose brat and he was hopping mad. He said he was inclined to arrest the whole bunch of them for interfering with his investigation and he would too if they didn't get their nets in the water and get out there and drag for that second body before the crabs ate all the evidence.

The harbor held forty shrimpers, innumerable deck-hands, and five fish houses (three on the east side of the harbor and two on the west side). The fishermen needed all five fish houses because fishermen liked their space. The wide-open bays of Texas had spoiled them rotten so they wanted pleeenty dragging space on the water and pleeenty docking space at the harbor with the crabbers over yonder and the gill-net fishermen tucked away on that dock. And the shrimpers! They didn't want nobody touching them or their stuff! Their worst nightmare was that another shrimp boat would rub up against their railing or that an idiot deckhand from the next boat over would climb onto their deck and check out their net and ask too many weird questions. Or worst of all, a shrimp boat leaving early in the morning and taking off half their rigging!

So the fishermen came and went at the docks with the exception of some old bachelor fishermen who never left the harbor. These fishermen couldn't tolerate the noise and close quarters of town and loved the only girls left in their lives—their boats—so they cooked in the cabin, washed out their old stinkin' blue jeans in a deck bucket, and hung them on the rigging or an oyster dredge to dry. At night they pulled down an old burlap oyster sack nailed over the window to keep out the moonlight and they got a little shut-eye.

Then when tragedy struck because the boat-bound fisherman went out to pee at night and in the process tripped over his dangling trousers, the docks was where his body was stretched out, and his dead blue face was just another blue thing on that wharf besides his denim trousers dangling around his knees.

Which wasn't the reception Sambo got. Sambo's gunshot wound was so messy and bloody that he was covered in a tarp and hauled straight from the boat to the back end of the truck. They totally eliminated the docks. Fishermen are oddly squeamish. They could gut and gill fish all day long, head a million pounds of shrimp, and sling their shrimp heads all over their feet and halfway across the docks. But let a fisherman drop a little blood on the docks and they were ready to puke their guts out. So nobody wanted to find Arch's body even though they believed (hoped) he might be alive. Well, maybe he was and maybe he wasn't. Stranger things had happened. Oh, who the heck knows? They got on their boats anyway (the sheriff was parked at the docks and directing the investigation from his car's CB radio) and drug not only the passes and reefs but all of Spirit Center and San Antonio and Hynes Bay. Day in, day out, sunup, sundown, the boats went out, the nets thrown over, drag drag drag. In between the drags, the shrimpers talked on the radio about that donkey of a sheriff sitting in his black car at the bay and the game wardens they hated worse than sheriffs and the sticks floating and the wrecks shifting and the ice melting and going to waste in their homemade ice boxes. Talk was the cheapest thing around when no money's being made and a shrimp net was dragging places no right-minded net ever would for a drowned body slick as trout vomit.

It all went to nothing. No body was found and Sambo's wife was pretty sure she wasn't even filing charges. Somebody did her a favor. So the sheriff got disinterested quick in a case going nowhere and redirected himself on a teenage beer break-in. The shrimpers sat at the dock, weary, disgusted, and questioning eight days of unlucky catches and who wanted to miss another day shrimping even if it was Archie Don they were lookin' for. Besides, no body! Now, what did that mean? Arch was probably livin' it up on the docks in Galveston. Or New Orleans. Why, just last month . . . wasn't it last month? . . . Archie Don was seen barefoot and in a tuxedo in Port Bolivar by a dozen shrimpers. In a tuxedo, mind you. And trotting along behind him in high heels was a fancy woman carrying a yapping poodle. Now, too dang bad about poor Sambo and we all feel bad about poor Sambo but we know we know Arch was . . . is . . . was . . . is (they couldn't make up their minds if he was alive or dead) a little different. He was the only shrimper they knew that could mess around a boat wearing only his underwear and rubber boots and nobody would think nothing of it. Nothing! Who cared? And that time Archie Don got ran over by a train outside the county line and got his front teeth knocked out, who did the women love more for it? Archie Don! They loved Archie Don.

Chief said he'd heard it all. He didn't believe that vanilla-wafer story about Archie Don being in Galveston. It didn't take a genius to see that Arch was dead. Not alive. 'Cause alive Arch wouldn't leave his boat in the hands of nobody—especially that fool Sambo. Why, last time Sambo was on the boat, Arch told him to steer for the light while he took a little shut-eye and Sambo steered for the light all right. He steered the boat clear up on the beach! The light was on the dang beach! Hellfire, boat people are funny anyhow, and Arch wasn't a bit different. They don't run off and leave their boats. They'd sit in a lake of

hellfire if they could sit on a boat. Just ask any preacher
in town and see if he don't tell you the same thing in a
hellfire second. And Chief wasn't even gonna discuss them
no-count Flordonian shrimpers—wasn't that where that
dang game warden who's wife Sambo was messing around
with come from? Flooorida? Hell! They ain't even in the
same ballpark. None of them stay around long enough for
anybody to figger them anyhow. Tear up a boat and they're
gone. Vamoosed. Dump the couch and all the kids in the
back of the truck and burn ever' bridge leaving.

It was day eight of the murder and I forget who all was
down in the engine room with Daddy, but I was the only
one up with Chief. The sun was shining on the deck, sun
sun sun. Like that. Not far off a seagull eyeballed a rotting
catfish floating belly-up. When the shrimpers first came
by, heading down below to talk with Daddy, they patted
Chief on the shoulder in the passing, but he brushed them
off. "I see y'all. Don't think I don't! I got spirit eyes and I
know quitters when I see 'em."

They patted Chief. Now now now, ol' man. We don't
doubt your feelings. But Arch ain't the first fisherman gone
missing and he ain't liable to be the last neither. We've seen
plenty boys go down the drink. Drug for them all, too.
Remember that boy in the hailstorm? We drug for him.
Found him. Then that man and his wife with a boatload of
oysters! The sky stinkin' with a fresh norther and blowing
the woman's hairpiece clean off her head! Heck, we found
the hairpiece 'fore we found her body! Dangest thing I ever
saw. Then those four fool boys coming through the jetties

in a squall. Remember that one? First the boat was there, then it was gone! WHAM! The water and wind jumping up and holding hands almost, with the boat dropping between them! A sure 'nuff circus act if you weren't blood-related to the poor things. Never did find them poor boys.

Truth was, Arch going missing was tiring out the shrimpers. So the only ones really left to be concerned were Archie's two ex-wives (nobody knew where they were) plus Chief and Daddy, who claimed Arch was his favorite brother. Troublesome, but favorite. Anyhow, that's what he told the other shrimpers when they came down and sat in his engine room, and I heard because I crept down (but kept my mouth shut). Chief didn't bother to come down; he just yelled through the hole at them. "A man wantin' his dead son back to bury him is natural as peaches falling off a tree! Hell, snow falling outta the sky! It's natural, you pack of dummies!"

The shrimpers rested their big brown wrists across their knees and leaned their heads into Daddy. Their boots weren't exactly in the engine grease but they were close. They heard ol' Chief all right but said, Billy, what we need to know is are *you* finished looking for Archie Don. Heck, they knew ol' Chief would never be finished. He'd probably try to pole the entire bay on that rotten skiff of his. Better watch out, Billy. Better watch out. That ol' man might give you some trouble yet.

Daddy said he had information he didn't want discussed—especially with a kid around—but he'd been in the Navy once and lost something and he guessed sometimes you just have to let things go. So he guessed he'd do the same thing again. Let it go. End the dragging. Arch was a bad dream full of twisting green tornadoes and he could be replaced even if he was a favorite. He had seven kids he could replace Arch with even if he couldn't remember their names right. And besides, who's to say Arch's even missing? Who's to say? Did the sheriff say it? Nope, he didn't! Maybe Arch was in Galveston. He sure hoped so. In the meantime, stop the dragging. Bad memories lived in the water or were buried out there or at least they were sitting in the sun, waiting on a ride in.

ONCE upon a time Daddy was a non–promise breaker, but that got flushed down the toilet when he was in the Navy. And him a married man too, Momma said. Today if a preacher announced in church that the Lord told him somebody was gonna give him three hundred dollars, Daddy would have jumped up (that's saying a lot—Daddy wouldn't have been in church) and said, "Not me, not me!" He certainly wasn't like he was in his holy-rolling younger days when he was drinking some glory-land juice that tobacco users, whiskey drinkers, tattoo addicts, dope gulpers, fornicators, murderers, and all liars could not drink. Then he'd have jumped straight up in his pew and afterward gone down to the fish house and wrote an IOU for the money he owed Jesus. If he didn't have the money, he'd sure 'nuff find a place to get it.

Whenever the subject of Daddy's backsliding came up, Momma always said, "Your daddy thought he was a perfect man. Oh my! A perfect man. Now, ain't that something.

Perfect, my eye! But wasn't no convincing him! Either he was walking on water like a prophet or he wasn't. All I'm gonna say is the higher they go, the harder they fall."

Besides, Momma wasn't convinced Daddy's sin in the Navy was all that bad. Probably wasn't more than any normal sailor would've done in a war if he had half the chance and his wife and kids were in another state. Drinking a beer in a bar or smoking a cigarette after he'd promised God he wouldn't. OR (and she'd just wager a bet on this one) carousing with some made-up Jezebel. That was just like a man. And your daddy a married man with three kids! But Daddy never said. More Secret City.

So not knowing for sure, Momma erected a half-dozen false stories with a little paper man that walked in and out of all of them. Daddy wasn't a Sears catalog paper man but he was pretty close. Then she dismantled her stories when it suited her the most, but mostly she was still angry that a married man with three kids would have *volunteered* for a war. Volunteered—while she stayed home with the kids. Now, if that don't beat the cake!

Actually the FALL boiled down to Grandma. If Grandma had left well enough alone. But oh no, she didn't. When Momma and Daddy started courting (and they'd been in grade school together so it was a long, drawn-out courtship), Grandma did her dead-level best to turn the tide against Billy Bones. Billy Bones was an unsaved tin-can bum. Billy Bones was an unsaved no-good fisherman.

Actually, Billy Bones wasn't Daddy's real name, but it was real enough to Momma, who was the captain of a pirate ship with Billy Bones the handsome, dashing mate. And he was a pretty good fisherman too, and he worked real hard on the weekends and at night when he wasn't in school. Didn't matter, didn't matter. Grandma was certain of the ripeness of God's harvest and the imminent and fiery end of all history, which she viewed with as much certainty as the fishermen viewed the daily rising and setting of the sun, so she and her family dared not falter. Especially after dead Delbert. Especially over a tin-can bum like Billy Bones, whose only aim in life seemed to be playing pirate games on his shrimp boat.

Momma wasn't willful. She hated conflict too much to be willful, but she was the smartest student in her graduation class of twenty and knew she wasn't gonna be a pirate captain long (with Billy Bones the mate) if she didn't get over that Rosa Belle hurdle. So their pirate games and minor courting started including more and more of Momma making salvation attempts on Daddy, telling him that Jesus loved him and didn't mind that nicotine on his hands so much. Jesus could wash that smoke off. Billy Bones just laughed. He was a bay and moon man. Paid lots more attention to dolphins sticking their noses out of the water and warning ever' fisherman around that gale winds were fixing to carve the town up like a turkey. Then too every weekend at sunup when he went shrimping, a million white and pink birds that laid all night in the marshes rose up and flew west with his boat. That was his church and he'd stake it against anything they had in that church of hers. Finally, though, to get her to quit preaching, Daddy made a deal with her that was so outlandish that, if it happened, it sure enough would be a sign from God. What else could it be? So Billy

Bones told Momma that if he caught two thousand pounds of *clean shrimp* (no fish, no jellyfish, no seaweed, just pure clean shrimp) in one drag, then he'd go to her church.

Billy Bones thought that was the end of it. After all, when was the last time a blue-eyed Jesus sent him a sign about anything? NEVER! Now, dreaming and signs was not an unknown or an oddity to Daddy. After all, he lived in the same household with Chief, who talked with spirits (alive and dead), and got daily instructions on the weather and bay conditions from dolphins and moon halos. Sometimes too a dream waffled in about traps to catch the armadillo that was burrowing underneath the front porch or how to trick shrimp into your net (dump a sack of cottonseed overboard).

Then one night Daddy dreamed two thousand pounds of shrimp waited for him along the edge of a mud hole in Mesquite Bay, so he took his shrimp boat to Mesquite Bay— clear across our bay and almost in another county—and he threw over his net and, sure enough, caught two thousand pounds in one drag. Daddy was nineteen—not a promise breaker yet—so he kept his end of the bargain with God, but, truth be told, he went willing. The prophetic dream was like a beam of light that shot down into his otherwise overcast horizon of a life and gave him sudden purpose and direction. Something other than shrimping, anyhow. Daddy went nuts for Jesus. He couldn't wait to get born again in the Church of Jesus Loves You. He couldn't wait to get anointed by the Holy Spirit, confess his sins, and get baptized at the bay with Grandma and her four girls and all the church watching. Overnight he became a changed man and swallowed the whole line of social sins: tobacco in all its forms, secret societies like Masons, life insurance, doctors, medicine, liquor, dance halls, theaters, movies, Coca-Cola, public swimming, professional sports, beauty parlors, jewelry, church bazaars, Christmas trees, and the entire idea of Halloween. He reined in his cussing too, only saying words like *dab gum* or *got dang* or something to that effect, and he quit smoking. Cold turkey. He couldn't do enough for Jesus. Give him a broom and he'd sweep under the church pews. So everybody in church knew and remarked and wondered. My my, God was sure working behind the scenes. Next the church elders elected Daddy the youngest deacon in the church and every Sunday morning he taught the young men's Sunday school class and every Thursday evening he directed the Boy Scouts of America in Indian ways.

That was conviction to Grandma and cemented her belief that Daddy was saved and a Holy Roller and a changed man. And it looked like it too, because after marrying Momma and their first Christmas together, Daddy wouldn't allow a Christmas tree in the house and forbade pants on Momma. That was the end of her pirate career. And Billy Bones too. That name was retired and was only brought up during Momma's baby-coming deliriums.

SIX

The shrimpers went back to dragging—for shrimp this time—and they had a whole lot of catching up to do because after all was said and done Archie Don was born in a town where fishing seasons mattered more than men gone missing. And it looked like a good fall shrimping season. Cold weather hadn't run the shrimp out of the bay. It hadn't even shifted the tree colors yet, except for the Chinese tallow and those worthless trees would turn yellow on a dime if their feet touched a thimbleful of ditch water. So it was a funny kind of mulled-cider season with a moon full of possibilities and Daddy hardly had time to switch nets before Momma sidetracked him with some of Chief's foolishness.

It was a chance remark in a half-opened door. Momma was letting in Sister Jackson and the shortcut (Momma got the long version) to Sister Jackson's long story went like this.

Sister Jackson had two pretty daughters that she forced to wear home-dyed black panties since grade school, but that didn't work no more so she watched them day and night as only a member of the Nazarene church burned to the ground by persons unknown could. Sometimes she lay in a ditch and waited for them. Anyhow, Sister Jackson also did hands-on healing for chicken pox, earaches, stomachaches, warts, broken limbs, cuts, burns, snakebites, and cats with fits, and once she exorcised the devil from a killer hen that pecked everything in the chicken yard including its own feet. In her younger days (before her focus was ruined by her girls) Sister Jackson had raised a cold, stilled child from the dead. Sister Jackson never took credit for her successes but claimed her power originated from the Holy Ghost. It was all according to faith anyhow. If you got one-dollar faith and ask for a ten-thousand-dollar item, it ain't gonna work.

Sister Jackson was a part of a small but powerful praying circle that included Grandma, Sister Jesse (some claimed she was a witch but actually it was the black garb she wore that drew all the talk), and sometimes Momma too, but not so much anymore 'cause she had five kids underfoot and couldn't keep her focus good. Sister Jackson pulled Momma out on the porch and said she needed to tell Momma a little something, because checking the roads for her girls like she was (she was in the ditch), she had acquired some information and nothing but good southern manners and fine God-fearing parents had kept her from getting closer and hearing the whole thing from the horse's mouth. As it was, she was gonna have to guess, Jesus willing, what the men were saying.

It was Chief and the sheriff. Chief had the sheriff's car stopped and Sister Jackson reckoned the sheriff was used to this type of thing—always being waved down in the middle of the street; man, woman, and child coming to his window, leaning in, and pouring out their troubles. Telling the worst kind of misery.

Momma said yes, she reckoned so too. Then Sister Jackson said the sheriff wasn't talking, no expression on that man's face, just Chief leaning in the window and ever' now and then taking his hand and waving it around like he was fluttering it about or talking about the birds in the air or something like that, and Momma said, He wasn't talking about birds, Sister Jackson, and Sister Jackson said, No, Sister Goldie, I didn't think he was. Then the sheriff took out a filthy cigar. Oooh Jesus, help him with that filthy habit . . . oh, heavenly Father . . . and he lit the thing but had to yank his head waaay back 'cause that cigar smoke was sooo awful. . . . And as well it should be, Sister Goldie, and Momma (thinking of Daddy) said, Aaamen, Sister Jackson.

Well, truth be told, Chief *was* talking about the birds. He told the sheriff that he'd been waiting on his dreams. Looking for direction. What's what. That type of thing. Sure 'nuff, one night he dreamed the underbelly of a bird (dead souls always showed up as birds) flew east toward the sun and he told the sheriff that was where he would find Archie Don's body—buried half in and half out of the sand with his eyes open to the sun. Well, what was left of his eyes.

Sheriff said, How you know it's Arch, ol' man, and ain't just you dreaming about birds?

Chief said, Right right, he was thinking the same thing himself but the next night he dreamed he saw a little black vapor and he argued with it for a while until the vapor cloud shouted, "For God's sake, Dad! It's Archie Don! When you see that game warden next, just blast away with your shotgun!" Chief said he realized then that he was talking to Archie Don and that he didn't own a shotgun. Before that it was anybody's guess who that vapor was. Sheriff said Chief was sure complicating things for him because he couldn't remember where he stuck that murder file and a little black vapor accusing a game warden of double homicide was serious serious business.

Chief's problem (and everybody thought he had a problem) was a whole lot like Grandma's. He wouldn't leave well enough alone. Wouldn't let the sleeping dog lie. Nope, he had to yank that chain. Chief wasn't gonna sit around doing nothing when a sign had clearly spoken.

But the way it was looking to everybody else was if Daddy waited around long enough he could have his daddy missing, too. That would make him two! So Daddy took a hard measure of Chief: he was old and had an old boat that was covered in front but opened in back and kept out nothing. Not wind or rain. So what use was it? None. An invitation for disaster was what it was. So thinking to save Chief's life on account of him not letting well enough alone, Daddy hooked Chief's fishing skiff on the back of his truck and hauled it out into the middle of the pasture to sit with the wrecked car, and not only did the tall grass cover the truck tracks, it also covered the trailer like the boat had brought itself out there. It was the boat's idea.

Chief didn't have to make a move. The sea moved for him. (When you're aligned with the bay, funny things like that happen.) In a more robust time and when folks' minds weren't so cluttered with murder and mayhem, the windows would have been boarded up or at least nailed shut and the clothes strung from pillar to post across the vast backyard would have been brought in. And Chief's old boat that was covered in weeds and infested with poison oak and who knows how many rattlers would have been tied with a strong rope to a nearby mesquite tree or at least an anchor thrown over and hammered into the ground. But it wasn't a robust time.

The gulls flew low. A northerly haze turned the sky yellow and for three days the fishermen sat on boats and talked of weather and the magical things that gulls do. One man said it was not gulls at all but whirling sharks that warned of winds. That was a sure sign and the way they twisted in the air was the way the wind would blow. A few fishermen disagreed. The vital sign of their enemy, the shark, who ate holes in their nets, was not the direction of the wind but a warning of things to come. Something down the road and who knows what that thing was. Maybe someone should go out and ask the shark.

Then the rains came. The wind racketed from every direction it pleased and the sea went mad. The storm was a total surprise to everyone but Chief and the seagulls. Nothing was securely fastened down. Not the sheets on the line, the swing in yard, the gate on the chicken pen. The chinaberry tree in the front yard went in a sharp snap and left a six-foot-wide gaping hole full of mud and salt water. Then the bay pulled itself ashore, going into places it was not invited, then uninvited still, and moving backward, it took Chief's boat off the trailer and to the backyard and within ten feet of the bayou.

Soon as the yard was cleared of broken chinaberry limbs and the table righted and Momma either in the kitchen or the backyard, Chief saw his chance and took off to the bayou. I was supposed to be in school but wasn't and was paying for it dearly by hanging out sopping-wet sheets on the clothesline. I caught sight of Chief and before I had my thinking cap on straight I told Momma and she sent me straight down to the bay to find Daddy.

At the supper table that night, Momma said, "He will kill himself," and with no more fanfare than that, she got up and started collecting the supper dishes. Supper was over! Daddy was pretty aggravated. He was still hungry. Besides, he was tired from working out on the bay in the hot sun all day and especially after the storm had left chicken pens and fences and people's underwear strung all over the muddy bottom. Then coming home and dealing with Momma worrying about Chief wandering out to the bay and drowning himself. So he said to nobody in particular, "Let him go fishing again." And Momma said, "He will kill himself. And besides, it ain't fish he's after."

"Well," Daddy said, "a man can't live forever."

Chief told me later that he was resting his head against the iron bars on his bed when the plan formed. It was such a good plan that it got legs (likely Archie Don helped it grow legs) and starting walking around the room, checking to see if the old man's head was still on the iron bars, and if so, well, okay, because it wasn't Chief's body that needed to be up walking around (he needed the rest for what was to come). It was just the idea. Just the idea.

The idea said that tattletale girl, Silver, needed to be up

and walking around too, even if she was a snitch. So Chief got out of bed and walked over to the house and stuck his head in the screen in my bedroom window.

"Girlie," he said. "Hey, girlie."

I was dead asleep and out in the window where my two sisters had crowded me. When the moon was just right, we were one shadow on the wall, but tonight I was just me. "Girlie," he said to the shape in the window and I roused and stared at him.

"Whaaat!"

Shusysh shush. Then he leaned into the window screen and told me his plan. I could be a part and if I didn't tattle again, he would give me a genuine Spanish coin he found on Dagger Point. He pulled it out of his pocket and shoved it up to the screened window. It gleamed in the moonlight, all right, and was probably last remembering a Spanish captain and I was a poor substitute.

Grandpa's boat was tiny compared to Daddy's shrimp boat so it wasn't hard shoving it down the bank and into the bayou. The plan was we both climb in. So we both climbed in. Chief squinted at the moon and took a little bayou water in his mouth for wind direction, and then we headed out, poling on sticks Chief whittled out of willow trees. After poling some time in the bayou, then clearing into the shallow bay, we switched to oars. When we reached the deeper water Chief said he believed he was in the right spot. He sat on his heels and hit the side of the skiff with his oar. We waited a minute and Chief said, "You just watch, a porpoise is gonna jump. It jumps a lot different when he's playing. Now . . . you see him jumping straight up? He's saying, 'Watch me, brother, watch me. Tomorrow's wind is coming from this direction.' Now, right before a norther that same porpoise there, or maybe another one like it, will jump straight up like just then and pop its tail on the water in the direction that wind's gonna blow. Don't tell me those porpoises ain't smart enough to know where Archie Don's at. They've seen him. Just need to ask them proper, with a little respect, is all."

Chief leaned on his elbows and rested the oar on his knee. "Spinning sharks is another sign. They might be the fishermen's enemy and all, but the shark can give you warnings just like the porpoise."

"Daddy says they're just going after fish!"

"Oooh, your daddy knows less than I'll ever forget. . . . Does he know about the moon sayin'? . . . Or did he forget that one too? Why, just the other night the moon had a circle with a hole in it, showing the wind was gonna blow outta the south, and sure 'nuff, dang south wind today."

Chief said it ain't good to mess with the wind just to be messin'. No fooling around. Proper respect! Why, he knew an old old story but a true story about a boastful daddy and his boys going out in the bay. Now, this was in the days when it was all sails out there. No loud motors! Sails! *Comprende?* Anyhow, this here daddy was impatient too. Boastful and impatient. Two bad qualities to have on the bay. Anyhow, he threw two bits overboard and said, "Ol' Man Wind, give my boys a quarter's worth of wind." So it breezed up a little bit, but the daddy still hadn't shown off enough, so he says, more prideful than before, "Heck, Ol'

Man, give me a DOLLAR'S worth." And just as he said that and flipped four quarters into the water, their boat was coming round that cut into Spirit Center Bay and the boat flipped over and the only one saved out of the whole bunch was that daddy. Rest drowned in Spirit Center Bay. Now, why do you think they call it Spirit Center? Because all them little babies drowned. True story.

Then Chief forgot all that. He was a fisherman marking time with an oar and remembering what all he'd seen. Big bull drum, huge old beasts living in the sea and drumming their song, and he fished over them and was happy for the fish he caught and for the fish he didn't catch, and the remembering got so fierce that he yelled, "Pipe!" bigtime, and I took his pipe out of his flannel shirt pocket and stuck it in his mouth, but he didn't light it. He just clamped his teeth down hard on the stem.

SEVEN

The Church of Jesus Loves You was a washed-out, run-down, former Air Force barracks that the Air Force abandoned after they came down during the Big War and took over the island in the bay, scooting folks off, sticking down their own houses and offices and barracks, landing planes, dropping bombs on the sand dunes, and sometimes dropping bombs full of little particles on the bay to see how radiation drifted in the wind, saying, How does radiation drift in the wind, fellas? And the fishermen saying, Radiation drifts like feathers falling off a seagull.

Holy Rollers loved old things. Old raunchy military barracks, drugstores with rotten floors, honky-tonks that smelled of beer, bankrupt picture shows. Something into something else. They loved converting things and it didn't bother them in the least that the devil was the previous owner. Matter of fact, knowing that the folding chairs in our church were hauled from a picture show tickled the deacons to death. They sprinkled a little olive oil on the seat covers, prayed over and asked forgiveness of their past sins, then rededicated them as seats for the saints. Another worldly besotted thing won over to Jesus's side in a war where the devil doesn't play fair. The deacons didn't even bother to repaint the red movie-show chairs. Red was the color of Jesus's blood.

The church was one block from town and two blocks from the bay, and behind the church was a winding bayou (everything in town had the winding bayou behind it) where cattails hid water moccasins and frogs that the snakes ate for dinner. Sixth-grade bad boys called the bayou Fertile Creek and for good reason, but the cows didn't care. They wandered down and lapped at the salty water like it was crystal-clear springwater coming pure from a mountaintop. A little more, a little more, more more. Thinking this until they fell off the bank or wandered down to the bay and drowned. Stupid cows. Once I found a whole cow head with horns buried in the tide. It had died, stuck in the mud or something. I'd walk down there sometimes, no thinking to it. My feet just going that way. Then I'd sit for three hours at the only place I wasn't getting away from.

I wasn't getting away from church. I loved church, but mainly I loved Brother Bob. He was our regular preacher and my substitute dad, and next to Abraham Lincoln and Jesus I loved Brother Bob the best. He wasn't new at the preaching ball game neither. He was ol-timey religion and got his training after the Lord told him to get up off his can and go find himself a church. So he did and found it in Seadrift with the fishermen. And he went where his fishermen flock went. Sometimes his fishing flock went down to the beer joint so there he went, too, with the beer-joint door wide open to the shell road and the seagulls and whatever or whoever else wanted to wander in. Brother Bob talked salvation. And the fishermen sat with their fists wrapped around cold dark bottles of beer and nodded. They all agreed. They'd seen Jesus out there on the bay a time or two. One saw him in a squall green as an unripened tomato. Twister weather.

Brother Bob didn't drink the beer. That was always suspected and gossiped over by loose-lipped, backstabbing saints, but he didn't drink the beer. What he loved were kids and magic tricks and soft belly parts of the Bible (mainly Psalms and Proverbs and Ecclesiastes where ol' King Solomon said somebody's toes were sparkling diamonds). Every Sunday morning, come hell or high water, Momma and all of us kids went to church. Daddy didn't come, but Daddy didn't count. He had backslid into his miry pit of tar and nicotine. Sunday was for preaching and praying and singing and folks getting counted and little cardboard numbers getting stuck up on the church attendance record. But the early morning was especially for kids. It was our time. For the two-year-olds, the favorite story was *The Good Shepherd*, and it had a game where one kid was the shepherd and two kids were the sheep and the rest were wolves who hid behind chairs while the sheep crawled around on the floor, baaing ever' once in a while until suddenly the wolves jumped out from behind the chairs and tried to eat the sheep (baaing furiously!) and the shepherd came running and whacked the wolves on the back.

Then there were Bible questions:

Bubba, who is Jesus?

He's God's little boy.

Bubba, where do Jesus and God live?

They all live in heaven.

Bubba, who are your two fathers?

God and my daddy.

For the older kids and teenagers, who were the devil's

chief target, there were more serious lessons to contradict all those stories we were hearing outside of church that was knocking us off the straight-and-narrow path. Our geography lesson went like this:

God ruled over a vast angelic empire that was divided into different orders of angels, and each moved in its own sphere. God sat at his throne in the center and the highest archangels had their thrones nearby and alongside them were angels of inferior orders. Commands came from the throne, passed to the archangels, then on down the line to the lesser angels, who sped off on their missions. Lucifer was the greatest archangel in God's empire and he lived on a perch up near the center of the universe. Originally he was God's chief angel, but he turned against God and was getting to be a big headache to God so God cast him down from his high position and as a punishment sorta carpet-bombed Satan's quadrant of the universe, the earth. (Defects in some planets can be traced back to this bombing.)

The earth existed for many millions of years in this semi-destroyed state, which was long enough for all the geological development claimed by scientists. Then God decided it was time to rebuild the earth. There was a big burst of activity on this old earth that had been only a mineral kingdom. Now God filled it with living plants and animals, and even though God sometimes worked slow on his creations, he was seriously concerned that this new work be done in a hurry. So God made a new earth in six 24-hour days.

Earth would last forever. God did not build earth to destroy it. God didn't build man to destroy him either. He was the peak of God's creative work. But Lucifer, who was the biggest angel headache of all time and not really an angel anymore but a devil through and through, was the leader of the Antichrist, whose chief goal was to tattoo the mark of the beast (666!) on everybody's earthly forehead or hand. Our chief goal as little soldiers in God's Earth Army was to trust in the Lord with all our might and lean not into our own understanding, and he would make our path a straight shot to heaven.

After Sunday-school lessons, the kids were turned loose to go back to the main part of the church where Brother Bob did the water-into-grape-juice trick. *(No wine! Unfermented grape juice!)* He spread his big white handkerchief over a big jug of water and little cups and the grape juice was somewhere hidden or maybe it was a white pill of some sort that turned the water into grape juice. When that trick was over, Brother Bob told everybody to line up in front of him to get some juice and crackers. But Brother Bob was pretty loose on details so the line was never in the right order with the brothers first, then the sisters, then the teenagers. Nope, the little kids ran down there first thinking it was penny marching time (they had their pennies in their hands) and the old brothers and sisters didn't mind, they were thinking the little kids were cute and handed them extra pennies out of their pockets and Brother Bob handed them a cracker too, so the kiddies ran back up the aisle screaming and eating crackers.

The penny march wasn't serious stuff, but Brother Bob said Jesus welcomed whoever welcomed little kids in his name, so that was plenty reason (plus the fact that sixteen pennies laid side by side measured a foot and a mile of pennies was worth $844.80!) for Brother Bob to dedicate thirty minutes to kids marching around the picture-show chairs with their pennies clutched in their hands while the guitar pickers and the fiddlers and Sister Pearl on the piano played a very loud and boisterous rendition of "Onward, Christian Soldiers." If there were enough kids, the penny march turned into a contest between the boys and girls to see who could get the most pennies for the missionaries in the field.

Then the arm slinging and marching turned into outright foot stomping and yelling with the old brothers and sisters on the chairs singing out and laughing loud and praising the Lord (hallelujahing), and sometimes they hopped fast over the entire row of picture-show chairs in an inspired moment to dump their pockets or their purses or untie their handkerchiefs to hand over all their nickels and pennies to the kids tearing up the church, marching for Jesus. Sometimes the penny contest got so loud and uproarious that Brother Bob had to take the jars of pennies and carefully and separately weigh them on a big scale he kept in his office and declare a winner.

After the penny march, Brother Bob gave a very low-key, nonhellite-type sermon that ended around one o'clock, and then the sisters fixed a fried oyster, fish, shrimp, or crab (depending on the season) dinner with red beans and potato salad and corn bread and fried okra and peach and dewberry cobblers and laid it all out on homemade quilts under a chinaberry tree that was trying hard to die but couldn't. The men saints sat around like they do (the women saints were in the kitchen part of the church), talking with their

Bibles lying down near their plates, the edges ruffling like the wind's thumb was licking them, and trying their best to ignore all the kids running around, screaming their heads off. Usually a sister stopped the screaming by tearing out of the kitchen and threatening all manner of stuff, and, before they got away, whacking them with a peach limb.

When Brother Bob wasn't preaching or weighing pennies or sitting in the beer joint and saving souls, he was praying the drowned fishermen into heaven. He said he never saw a dead fisherman he didn't like. At funerals where a preacher had a captivated audience and a dead person he could send wherever he pleased (to hell, for instance), Brother Bob sent the dead to the heavenlies. It was the last thing the family heard, anyhow, and caused lots of relief and members quitting and joining our church. He was a no-hell kinda preacher, bordering on Methodist, and that's why he was in trouble. He wasn't preaching "hard shell" enough, so our Air Force church was dead as a hammer.

None of the complaints had come up while Brother Bob was preaching. Oh no, the complaints came up because Brother Bob had gone to Seguin to cut firewood because Seadrift was a town that couldn't afford a preacher even if it wanted to. So the complaints piled in with a few vocal backstabbing saints leading the fray and I was sitting next to the church window and heard it all. I also could see every little thing long before it showed up at the front door, so when two men in a Chevy truck drove up in the church yard, parked in the high grass, and slung open the truck doors, I thought they'd drag up a rattlesnake for sure, but they didn't. They tromped straight in, one brother leading another brother, and both breathing hard like they couldn't wait to meet starving saints with nothing in their dead Air Force church but rotten bananas to eat. We were minus Brother Bob to defend himself. It wasn't fair but it was okay with them. It was just jim-dandy with them because gossip had reached fever pitch about beer drinking and beer joints and preaching easylike in a time when Jesus needed holy machine gunners.

Sitting in a church on Saturday wasn't normally something Momma did. She was waaay too busy cleaning house and hanging wash and making dinner and ramrodding seven kids. Plus the church door wasn't open on Saturday unless it was revival week. And it wasn't revival week. Momma didn't go to church on Wednesday night neither. Nobody went except Brother Bob, his wife, a couple deacons, Sister Pearl, a brother with a shrimp boat named *Salvation*, and Sister Lout in the back row with her shoes kicked off and the heels of her feet black as potatoes dug from the dirt.

So today was different. It was an emergency, and standing at the pulpit with his hand on his hip was black-headed Brother Beller (the visiting evangelist with the missionaries and the dead singers!)—trying to be Brother Bob.

He said, "Y'all heard any tongue speaking lately? Nosiree! Nobody's heard speaking in tongues since who knows when and the Bible's real clear about tongues. If it ain't happening then God ain't there. The devil is. Oh yes oh yes, the devil. Now, there are many many kinds of devils. Devils that get men killed. Devils that steal from the church . . . oooh they love to do that. And Lord help y'all on that one. Then there's the devils of witchcraft, fortune-telling, smoking, drinking, laziness, cussedness. Y'all know them! Yessiree. Then there are whining devils, yelling and screeching devils. There are demons that possess lawn-mowers and automobiles and chickens. There are devils that cause saints to run around the house naked or climb into windows for no good reason. The worst devils of all, though, are those devils that show up when tongue speaking has disappeared in the Lord's house. . . . And oooh, Jesus, help us here. . . . 'Cause these devils sometimes FAKE a good church. Only it ain't a good church—it's a dead church. And that's what we've got ourselves here.

"Now, y'all are probably thinking, oooh, the devil ain't that alert. After all, he is the devil and the devil has many qualities but smarts ain't one of them. Well, don't y'all believe that, brothers and sisters. Don't believe it. The devil is mighty smart, and the only thing that will cut his smartness in half is y'all praising Jesus in the spirit. The Holy Spirit! Speaking in tongues! Hallelujah!"

For the people in the know (evangelists wandering in and out of tent revivals or little brush arbor meetings here and there, preaching something from the back end of a truck or in somebody's backyard, preaching in the church) speaking in tongues was the Lord of the universe's way of speaking to his people. It was a sign that the Lord was dwelling inside you and every time the Lord wanted to play his personal piano he just tuned up the vocal cords of his handiest saint and played with his own fingers—speaking or singing any language he wanted.

Sometimes tongue speaking could happen without warning. Like when a highfalutin' man came to a tent revival and tried to throw scorn on something he thought sounded like barnyard chickens cackling. Well, that wasn't barnyard chickens. That was the Holy Ghost doing whatever he wanted. So without warning, the Holy Ghost could strike this high and mighty man down and in a short while he would be wallowing on the dirt floor, babbling in a foreign language.

I sure hoped I wouldn't be wallowing in the dirt, but I didn't know. The closest I ever got to speaking in tongues was when Daddy's shrimp boat got to rocking and a-rolling in a squall and the shrimp tubs and the shovel were flying across the deck and I nearly got washed overboard. I got so excited and gibberish that Daddy sent me down to the engine room to cool off. Another time a cold blue norther pushed across the skies and rolled dark clouds like a smoky coin—some parts hard and shiny as a nickel and other parts wide as a quarter—and the norther pitched lightning and threw chairs and leaves and buckets all over the yard and I flung myself backward in the grass, my arms and legs twitching, my hair flying everywhere, and shouted words that made no sense. Sheena, my sister, said I sure sounded like a Holy Roller to her and it took Momma two hours to get the sticker burrs out of my hair.

Brother Beller said, No more Mr. Nice Guy. He was getting to the nitty-gritty.

"Folks, I'm not gonna be y'all's friend tonight. Nosir. Nosir. Say it to me, folks. Not gonna be y'all's friend tonight."

We all said, "Not gonna be our friend tonight."

Somebody stuck his hand in the air. "Oooh, help him, Lord."

"I was conversing with y'all earlier. . . . And bless y'all sisters' sweet heart for such a wonderful meal, but tonight I'm a soldier in God's army, and hallelujah, I'm on that Great Battlefield between Good and Evil and I'm gonna tell y'all straight like the Holy Scripture says. Behold the way is narrow and few shall enter there. And RIGHT NOW, saints. This church is goin' to hell if it don't get straight with the Lord-uh. Am I right or am I wrong? Say it, folks!"

"He's right, Lord. He's right."

"Yeeesss-uh. I can feel it in my bones, Lord-uh. I feel you talkin' to me. Praise be his precious name. Folks are going to hell because this church is stone-cold dead. IT'S TWICE DEAD! Satan has plucked it out by the roots and it is utterly without spirit. Now, Brother Beller, y'all say, how can brothers and sisters of a LIVING Jesus Christ be sitting in a DEAD church? Y'all sayin' that. I see that sister over there—bless yore heart, sister—saying, Brother Beller, how can folks of a LIVING Jesus Christ be sitting in a dead church? How is that possible? Well, I'm gonna tell y'all. A church goes dead when Satan's pretend saints . . . yeeesss, I said that right! Y'all heard me right! Satan's pretend saints! That's you, brother, so quit lookin' at me like you ain't. . . . Can't give up their doctrines and opinions, their devilish and fiendish ideas . . . and oooh, brothers, when y'all's shrimpers believe a woman matters more than Jesus Precious Blood that died on Calvary matters . . . weeell, somebody's going to hell. Did that upset you?

Talking about y'all's shrimpers that way? Well, saints, when fishermen are out there on the bay killing each other . . . and lovin' women that AIN'T THEIR WIVES . . . whyyy, I can't prettify that abomination any more than that. Oooh, I can hear y'all sayin', 'Now, Brother Beller, fishermen in the Bible were Jesus's brothers and his lowly disciples. Have a little respect, Brother Beller. Have a little respect.' Well, boohoohoohoo, in the house of the Lord killing each other is a sin. An abomination. Why, there's a commandment about it! And not TITHING to the Lord. Oh, thieves and robbers! Thieves and robbers. 'Cause . . . and listen to me on this, saints! Not supporting your church is the same as stealing from the Lord's plate. That's an abomination too, brothers and sisters. TWICE AN ABOMINATION and that smells like rotten fish in the nostrils of God!

"Oh, don't even begin to feel sorry for yourself and think you got it bad. Quit your crying. 'Cause in the olden Biblical times, hate was a lot worse. Whyyy God's folks, the Israelites, spent thirty-eight years alone with him in the wilderness. Having church with him every day, ark in their midst, daily sacrifices, clouds of fire, men talking face-to-face with the almighty! And what did they get for all that? God wiped them out 'cause they disbelieved, and that is why there is no Holy Ghost hovering here wanting to give y'all ANYTHING. Certainly not the gift of tongues. NO siree!"

Finally he stopped and wiped his face with an oily handkerchief and lifted his head and pleaded to the ceiling, "Leave your mind at the door, folks! Check it in tonight, 'cause y'all won't be needin' it, praise Jesus's precious name. It will only get in the way and trip you up. . . . And oh how strange and wonderful it is."

Then he whispered in a low raspy voice that sounded like it was fixing to give out that he was gonna give a little altar call and ask the Holy Ghost to come in. "Forget all that name-calling. Never mind that. Because oooh, brothers and sisters, the Holy Spirit is a beautiful thing when it happens, so don't get scared. It's just Jesus wanting to marry you. To take you up as his bride and sit with the wedding party in heaven.

"And that ring—that beautiful engagement ring—is speaking in tongues. That's Jesus's engagement ring. Now, some folks might get embarrassed and want to hide that ring in their pocket like a handkerchief they just wiped their snotty nose on. That is a very dangerous thing to do."

He asked a sister that didn't normally play the piano if she wouldn't mind coming up to the piano and playing a little. "It don't matter, sister. You can play. Praise Jesus. Y'all too, brothers with the guitars. Y'all come on down with those guitars."

And they all came, watching their feet, careful not to look up and give the preacher a sign that they were needing saving. They had backslid, too. Another night, Lord. Another night.

"Now, close all y'all's eyes and all heads bowed."

So we bowed our heads and closed our eyes and I peeked but didn't see nothing but the hard line where my eyelids met. Brother Beller (more rasping, his voice was clearly giving out) said, "If the Angel of the Lord takes one of y'all tonight in a terrible head-on car collision . . . are y'all ready? Are y'all?" He sure hoped so. "Everybody knows Satan's snares and how you could unwittingly sin and backslide and what you thought you once had, you now had lost. Sinning willfully, though, is worst 'cause that's gonna put you in an awful position on that head-on car collision. You better get right, folks. You better get right, because if you don't, that's DENIAL and denial, my brothers and sisters, is an insult to the Holy Spirit and for that man, woman, OR CHILD will be damned forever in a everlasting pit of fiery hell.

"Folks, you don't know hot! Folks, I believe in a hell hotter than the Baptists teach. I believe in a hell hotter than your own former pastor preached. I believe in hell that utterly destroys the wicked. Only destruction will satisfy all that justice demands, and God, if he be a God of love, justice, and mercy, will ask no more of us than that the wages of sin be death.

"So come on down, folks, and pray out your denial right now! Pray that the Holy Ghost will come!"

If all the dirty feet in the world decided to wash up at the same time, the time was now and the altar was the water we were rinsing in. I was wanting my feet washed. Oh Lordy Lordy, I wanted them washed. I was in such despair for a washing that I imagined blisters popping out on my feet. Jesus poked me in the ribs too, saying, Come on, sinner. Come on down. Tomorrow will be too late. I will find your useless life and make it oatmeal.

There was nowhere to hide. No trees leafy enough or

weeds high enough or water deep enough. Jesus had found my hidey-holes so I slid to the floor and laid my head flat against the picture-show chair and the tears welled from my eyes and pasted my face to its red oily surface. I could taste the salt in my mouth. Then God or Jesus or, I don't know, maybe the Holy Ghost poured me into a little heap of useless powder on the floor and warned me if I moved an inch without getting myself born again, he would blow me into a fiery furnace. The time was now. The time was now. Nine years old don't mean nothing to God.

The sister was playing the piano pretty bad, but the Holy Ghost was turning it into something pretty good:

> *You long have been liv-ing a-way from your God*
> *And sin-ning a-gainst the light.*
> *You've trav-eled a rough and a dan-ger-ous road,*
> *Come back to your savior tonight.*

Brother Beller bawled out, "All you sinners out there. Raise y'all's hand. Y'all know it! All eyes closed now. Raise it, brother. Yeeesss-uh, I see you. I see you. Praise the Lord-uh. Come on down here, brother. The Lord's waiting—waiting on you-uh. Will y'all hear his call? Oooh Lord, make our hearts soft. Oooh Lord, give us softness of the heart. That is a good disease in Pentecostal time. A hard-hearted fella can't get it."

Somebody cried out, "Blood blood blood blood blood blood," and somebody else yelled, "Help us, Lord." Momma was crying and hanging on to Sister Pearl, who was waving both arms in the air. Hallelujah hallelujah.

Brother Beller stepped down from the pulpit. He was on the Lord's battlefield now and he walked like a serious doctor tending some seriously wounded folks. He made his rounds with a little bottle of olive oil and a big handkerchief out of his back pocket and every time he put his hand on a sinner's head to bless them or helped them through to conviction, he doused oil over the handkerchief and held it over the person's head.

He walked over and laid his handkerchief on Sister Pearl's head. "Shambalaleeleeeee, TAKE HER, LORD! TAKE HER!" Sister Pearl fell over backward and her braided hair came tumbling down. Next he reached over to Momma, who was hunched over and crying in her picture-show chair, and he pressed his handkerchief against her face and shoved her back against the seat and she fell, wide-eyed and looking stunned. Brother Beller warned us, "The Holy Spirit is moving, folks. Don'cha hear the mighty wind? Saints, say ya hear it, ya hear it! It's a rushing of a mighty wind."

I wept and wailed at my chair, praying my little heart out and getting born again, getting rededicated, getting Sister Pearl's hanky on my head while she called me her Little Angel Missionary. Then when we got home, Momma boasted to her evil brood that had stayed home with Daddy to watch TV that Silver got the bridal bouquet from the Holy Ghost. Sheena and Pill were instant in their response. "Haaaaa . . . ," they howled, and their eyes flashed like guns loosed. "Whoooo will you maaarrry? Whooo do you luuuv? Will you maaarrry Jesus? Brother Beeeller?" They finally stopped when I crawled under the kitchen table and burned myself on Daddy's cigarette that was dangling from his fingers. For that little mishap, even my brother who burned my Sears-catalog paper dolls left me two quarters on the floor. Too late, too late. I went to the bathroom and jerked the towel rack off the wall, then I climbed through the window and went out and sat in the dead-dark car where yellow jackets were ramming their heads against the closed windows. I was waiting for the wedding in the air.

I was starting to confuse myself.

EIGHT

In a bay flush with boats, talk about game wardens killing fishermen overtook the sticks-in-the-water discussion on the radio. Chief started it, but what the heck. Fishermen hated game wardens, anyhow, so it was an easy subject to spend hours on, arguing if the game wardens were on the bay or not, if they were in a good mood or not, and if somebody had seen their skiff, was that somebody ticketed all ready?

There was always a steady stream of game wardens in town. Get used to one unfriendly ugly face, then Austin sent another one, driving a dark green truck like he was heading for the forest instead of the bays. But green was okay with some game wardens. Green would hide them in the shinnery and the oak trees. Well, not actually hide them 'cause they didn't need to hide. They were bold as brass sitting in their trucks in plain sight of the docks and the fish house, and on the worst days sitting on the edge of the canal waiting for a shrimp boat to come along and hand them their prearranged FREE tub of shrimp. Free for not hassling them. Free for not handing them a hundred-dollar ticket. It was an understanding of sorts. Blackmail of sorts. You gotta pay for inattention from the game warden. Nothing was free on the bay.

The game warden Chief was charging with double homicide wasn't from Seadrift, but probably someplace close. Probably Florida. A Flooordonian with a gray skiff that was the same color and disappeared on the water just like Daddy's. A shrimper could be lookin' across the bay, seeing nothing on the flat gray water, just flat gray water, then, *boom!* There was the game warden with a ticket book.

Most game wardens had the decency to act uneasy around a fishing town. They'd get on their skiffs or ride down a dusty oyster road to the fish house in their trucks like it was the strangest thing they'd ever done. Sure wasn't their home. Wasn't even close. Only safe thing about coming into this fishing town was their gun riding a hip.

But not this game warden. They knew this type of guy. His folks were probably fishermen or else he was poor all his life and was trying to make up for it on the backs of fishermen by meeting at least one shrimper a week out on the canal with his little deal: a tub of shrimp for one day he didn't mess with you. Maybe two if he wasn't feeling good. So shrimpers made one drag just for the game warden because it cost a shrimper less that way than if he took a day off to complain to Austin, whining over the telephone about a dishonest game warden. He stole my shrimp! He stole my shrimp! Oh, pooey, Austin would say. You bunch of lying shrimpers. We don't believe you lying outlaw shrimpers. And forget the sheriff. The game warden business was no business of the sheriff and that was pretty much what the sheriff told Chief.

So Chief quit talking to the sheriff and he quit talking with the shrimpers because they thought Archie Don was gonna show up any weekend with a Louisiana woman on his arm anyhow. Archie Don was having a little harmless fun was all. The shrimpers' argument was, Why wart the sheriff over the game warden? Why stir up trouble? And sure, the game warden probably killed Sambo, but Sambo had it coming. They lived in a big ol' state of Texas where husbands shot their wives' lovers all the time and got nothing but congratulations for it. Sometimes they shot their wives, too.

So Chief holed up on his boat he had hid on the bayou behind a bunch of cattails and said he wasn't gettin' off. Not sliding back to the land like a lizard. Even if the dirt was where he was born, it wasn't where he was returning. So nobody knew for sure when Chief's fishing skiff left because in a town swarming with boats, nobody knows for sure when one leaves.

So Momma made another trip to the bay and told the fish house man to get Daddy on the radio and warn him about Chief, so the fish house man called Daddy, saying, "Billy, your old man is running around the bay, looking for Archie Don. Or that got dang game warden. Or both."

Nothing amused shrimpers more than other shrimpers acting crazy, so even though the killings were a tragedy, they had comic overtones and everybody at the docks had a big laugh over Chief and Daddy. Daddy chasing Chief and Chief chasing the game warden. Heck, they'd already cracked up about one local shrimper that had hauled off to a back bay and was rumored to be run over by a tugboat in the night with half the Calhoun County game wardens waiting for his body to resurface, when he showed up in town with a hangover and a tan and spoiled the whole thing.

Chief returned under his own steam with no thanks to Daddy. And he was right. Archie Don was dead and there was a body to prove it. So Archie got a second grave and it took all evening and a stick of dynamite because Daddy, feeling guilty, made sure the grave was square and deep and the mound of dirt that was dug from the hole was covered with a quilt so folks standing nearby didn't have to see Archie's coffin and the hole and the dirt too. A two-month floater was plenty terrible, even for fishermen who saw dead shrimp and fish on their back deck all the time.

The cemetery was fenced on all four sides with barbwire to keep out cows and wild hogs, and behind one side was an old peanut field where kids built forts and threw hard chunks of dirt like snowballs, and when that war making was done they'd shimmy up the old toothless limb of a big grapefruit tree that was the only tree living where twenty years ago there were dozens and they'd eat ten grapefruits in a sitting.

Most of the fleet showed up at the gravesite. Fishermen, crabbers, and shrimpers. It wasn't oyster season so there weren't oystermen. There was a huge amount of guilt to go around since everybody had doubted Chief, and Archie Don's death. Nobody had really wanted to see him dead. So they came to say their final good-byes and regrets about not returning that engine part they borrowed. Or that net they borrowed. Then too they wanted to tell Chief they were sorry and what a good ol' guy Archie Don was.

So the graveyard was full and me and my sisters, dressed in identical navy blue dresses cut from the same grocery sack pattern Aunt Teny had dreamed up two days before, were shoved from underneath the chinaberry tree that was giving a little shade and out into the sun. The flies were zapping around my head and I didn't even want to think where they had landed first. Then Brother Beller arrived and I knew it wasn't gonna be a friendly service. Chief was surprised and Daddy acted confused too, but they both knew Momma was probably at the bottom of it since Momma liked Pentecostal preachers and Brother Beller was the next real thing with Brother Bob gone. Which was exactly what she said. Brother Bob was gone to Seguin so who, pray tell, could they get? Some beer sot from the honky-tonk? Chief spat on the ground and said he wished he'd left Arch out on the beach to become a sand dune. Hell a mile, he might still drag him out there! Daddy better post him a girl out on Archie's grave tonight!

I wasn't a bit worried. Daddy wouldn't stick us out there in the dark in a graveyard and Chief wasn't gonna drag Archie anywhere. He was too weak for that kinda digging. Besides, the cemetery was dead center of a pasture chockfull of devil's head cactus with big thorns saying, Oh yes oh yes, I am food for your foot. He'd have to get through that first.

Then I took it all back because Brother Beller said he was inviting the cows coming through the peanut field to come in and eat the lovely grass growing around Arch's grave. There wasn't nothing the Lord abominated worse than grass growing around a sinner's feet when it ought to be devil's head cactus.

Momma's final comment over Archie was, "Man's short life ends and things go on." It wasn't from the Bible; it was something she made up to shorten conflict in her life. Because Momma hated conflict. Then she went home and took the iron bed my baby brother was born in and hauled it out in the yard. She jerked the iron legs off the bed and flipped the mattress upside down under a cottonwood tree, then she got a broom and a mop bucket full of kerosene and handed it to me, saying, "Kill ever' chigger livin' and hidin' in that bed." It took the rest of the day with the iron legs laying in the sun and the mattress upside down under the tree before she'd say it was done. At nightfall, she drug the iron bed back in and I got a dull headache from all the kerosene I was smelling underneath the bed. I saw Archie in the dust. Falling from the rusty bedsprings.

Chief took off to the fish house. He was on a tangent. He questioned every shrimper that came in on the whereabouts of that Flooordonian game warden, and some of the shrimpers patted Chief on the shoulder, telling him how bad they felt about Archie and that dang game warden that dang game warden, then they walked off to their trucks and went home to supper. The day was finished for them. Others were not so fast to let their day of ruination end. They were polite men, anyhow, and would sit for hours on each other's boats, talking about the full moon and the high tide and should the shrimp be stirred or just better left alone. They took turns with the water hose and the gasoline hose like they were first cousins on a sleepover. Let me help you patch that net. Let me run that cable for you.

Then they realized that Chief wasn't getting off his game warden tangent. Hell, nope! He was trying to arrange a semiposse or at least reopen an investigation, so they just stood there, standing on one leg awhile, then switching legs. What would it cost them to listen? So they stayed and stayed. Not joining any posse, just something different from the boat for a change.

Daddy's biggest headache after the funeral wasn't that Brother Beller sent Archie to hell twice (once for his double marriage and another for getting himself killed). Nope. It was the reverse kinda thinking that Chief did when his baby brother died in the fire. Wasn't the daddy; it was the wind! So Archie's dying wasn't because a game warden went berserk on the bay or Sambo's bad luck finally outrun his good. It was the water! And what luck the town faced it, so it was a whole lot of water for Daddy to fret about. Daddy said from now on there wasn't gonna be no more swimming in the rice canals or jumping off bridges into the bayou or lounging on the bow of the shrimp boat where kids sprawled from the tip end of the bow all the way to the cabin window with their feet nearly in his mouth. Nooo, because guess what was the first thing that boat propeller would run over if he ever hit a reef? Liable to be our stupid little heads.

Another thing Archie's death succeeded in was giving Daddy a double dose of game warden paranoia. Shrimpers catch it anyhow just being commercial fishermen, same as kids picking dewberries catch poison oak. It went with the territory. The high almighty game wardens. God might call the shots in church and in town but the game warden called them on the bay. That's what happened when state agencies got involved in fishermen's business and sent uniformed men with guns strapped around their hips to walk on their boats, uninvited, and ask them crazy questions like, What size shrimp? What size net? Where's your license, buddy? Or they'd drive their trucks across your front yard and talk to you from the window while you stood on the porch in your underwear, and if there was another game warden handy in the truck or on the skiff or just standing nearby—forget it. He said nothing. On automatic pilot.

Some shrimpers reduced fickle encounters with game wardens by hiding out in canals or back bays surrounded by submerged reefs until the game warden's skiff left the bay or was drug out of town on a trailer behind a truck. In prime-time shrimp season, men whose ever' waking moment was festering on unloading shrimp or culling shrimp or changing shrimp nets for the umpteenth time would suddenly drop anchor in a back bay. Then, bored out of their skulls and with the seabirds flapping and begging for food, they would toss bread crumbs from their leftover bologna sandwiches. Hiding out from the game warden was the one time in a fisherman's life when it was okay to be lazy as a hound dog and bask in the sun, drinking hot RC Colas by the caseload.

When Daddy went shrimping again his way of avoiding game wardens was more Secret City stuff: he left his truck and boat in a different spot every time and if it was to a back bay or a near one he was heading, he flat wouldn't say.

Only shrimping in a back bay (which was usually where he went) meant leaving earlier and returning to the docks later at night with mud and shrimp and hardheads all over the back deck because Daddy didn't have a deckhand to cull his shrimp, having lost his deckhand because what deckhand wanted those kind of crazy hours. So Daddy was both running the boat and culling the shrimp. That's when seven kids come in handy and I was the least complaining and easiest roused at four in the morning, so I was the early bird that got that shrimping worm.

On weekends, we left in the early morning hours and returned late at night. If a norther threatened to roar in and send the shrimp moving and boats scampering, I traded school for the bay and spent the night rocking on top of Daddy's shrimp boat with a blanket to cover me from the wind and the rain. Sometimes the wind blew so fierce that it sent my blanket out into the middle of the bay and shoved half the water off the flats.

On school days, I was pulled from the supper table when Daddy got to the docks. Momma handed me a hunk of corn bread with a little butter and told my brother to take me to the fish house. I could eat supper with Daddy later.

I was good as any little boy (or any man for that matter) about sticking my hands in mud and fish slime and not caring if jellyfish burned my arm or the shrimp and hardheads pricked my hands. There was always a green bottle of oily Campho-Phenique to take care of that problem. (It wasn't the same thing as red monkey blood but it was close.) I kept my mouth shut too, becoming a little invisible nothing with fast-moving hands, which was really what

Daddy liked best. He couldn't stand to hear a woman talk. Yak yak yak, he said. That's all y'all do. Yak yak yak.

We were culling a bad last drag full of mud and hard-heads and the docks were empty and dark except for a wire that Daddy ran through the rigging to light up the worst of the drag. We were sitting in a damp well hole. I was resting my tailbone on my heel bones and my hands and face and arms and knees were covered in jellyfish slime and shrimp vomit (shrimp don't really vomit, but there was a lot of stuff on the deck that looked like they did). I let out a loud weary moan. Daddy's response was to sling another bucket of bay water over the freshly culled tub of shrimp and tiny rivers of mud washed out the tub holes and settled down around my knees.

No complaining about the backbreaking work! No complaining, no complaining. As Daddy said, those that care a flip don't need to be told and those that don't care DON'T CARE. Still, I had high foolish hopes that Daddy would holler at me to cover the shrimp pile with oyster sacks and let the fish house boys take care of it in the morning. You've had enough, kiddo. That was my dream.

But nope, that wasn't happening 'cause even Flordonian shrimpers don't let their shrimp stay out all night in the mud and the gunk to get soft as boat grease in a crankcase. Quitting signal for Daddy was when ever' last shrimp was culled, washed three or four times, iced down with an oyster sack covering it, then left at the back door of the fish house until the wee morning hours when the fish house man arrived at the dock to unlock the fish house and found Captain Bill's shrimp sitting there. Then and only then was quitting time.

It was getting close though, 'cause Daddy threw a half-dozen wrinkled soft-shell crabs from the drag in a deck bucket and told me to go down by the oyster shells and clean them. So I went under the wharf and sat on my haunches with the soft crabs splayed out on the oyster shells in front of me like little fat Jesuses. I took my time. I didn't like ripping the crab shell open. I didn't like pulling the soft and hard little bits of something out of its belly. If a crab was REALLY REALLY DEAD I didn't mind so much, but if it was ALIVE and its little feelers moving, I'd imagine the tearing and the ripping of its little soft gut, the searing pain of a back cracked open. My high-fidelity imagination was probably why I was such a jim-dandy fast culler, too. I raced through every shrimp pile, pitching flopping fish and crabs and little blue-eyed blowfish off the deck as fast as I could get them because I hoped they'd hit deep water before the thundering swarm of seagulls sunk their claws into their tender flesh and hauled them off. *Wham wham wham!* Hardballs going over a home plate! *Wham wham!* More hardballs. But my hard slam dunks were probably killing them outright.

I was deep in life-and-death thoughts, investigating the crab's feelers with my finger, when a man walked out on the wharf. I could tell by the sound and looking through the cracks in the wharf that he wasn't a shrimper. He wasn't wearing rubber boots. Daddy was down in the engine room, doing the last thing he always did before he left the docks and went home—checking the stuffin' box in the engine room for water leaks—so he didn't see the man step on his boat. Otherwise he would have yelled, "Keep your cotton-pickin' feet off my boat!" (Shrimpers rarely if ever allow strangers to step on board their boats unannounced and uninvited.) So Daddy climbed out of the engine hole and there on his deck was a game warden wearing sunglasses at midnight and he wasn't smiling. The game warden hung his thumb over his pistol a minute, then he walked across the deck and stuck his boot on a tub of shrimp. He got to the point real quick.

"Out kinda late, ain't you, Cap?"

"Nawp," Daddy said. "It ain't that late."

"What size shrimp you got there? Look kinda small to me," he said and dipped his black toe in the shrimp and flipped them around.

"They're legal. Count 'em if you like. I ain't hiding nothing."

"Maybe. Maybe not," the game warden said. "Where'd you get 'em?"

Daddy wasn't quick answering that question because asking any shrimper where he caught his shrimp was like asking a man if you could look at his underwear. It wasn't polite and it wasn't done.

Daddy squinted his eyes and looked at the game warden like he was crazy. "These are legal shrimp. I already tole you."

"And I told you shrimpers to stay there on the east side of the reef. I told three or four of your buddies anyhow. . . . And I told them to tell the rest of y'all. So east side of the reef. That's where I want y'all. Ever' little friggin' mast pole."

"When did Austin get a law on game wardens givin' shrimpers directions?"

"Look, Cap, either you go where I tell you or you can go where you want, but the payback on that one is something to keep these little eye-peepers shut. You *comprende?* Or you could lose the whole damn load. I don't know. I don't know how I'll feel tomorrow. . . . Besides, you already got stuff workin' against you, Cap."

"What?"

"You got stuff . . . workin' against you. Can't you hear? Chief. Ain't he your old man? Well, if he is . . . then you got stuff workin' against you. Like I said. Might want to fix it before you start spoutin' off on decisions that might haunt you later on. *Comprende?* So which way you want it, Cap?"

"I shrimp where I please," Daddy said.

"Suit yourself, Cap, but you might wanna think again."

Then he was gone quick as he came and I climbed out from underneath the wharf with a deck bucket of dead soft-shell crabs and Daddy was still standing on the back deck. He hadn't moved. Finally, he looked at me and said, "THAT," and he pointed to the vanished game warden, "is one sunavabitch."

NINE

Daddy said lucky devils can outsmart game wardens. Lucky devils can do most anything if they don't yak about it to everybody under the sun before they do it. I was pretty excited about the idea of a good devil. In my short life I had yet to come across one of those, so in my astonishment that one of Satan's minions was actually helping us, I spilled the jelly jar of hot coffee wrapped in newspapers between my legs in the truck. But Daddy was cool as a cucumber and lifted his clean pair of shrimping clothes and three bacon and egg sandwiches that he'd eat on the way out to the back bay (the coffee was for whoever drank it first) out of the coffee mess and shouted for me to calm down. Calm down! We ain't done it yet!

It wasn't near daylight. Hours and hours yet to go. Only the sound of water moving over oyster shells and the early-bird shrimpers milling around on their boats, puttering with a rope or a net. Somewhere in the harbor a light in a cabin came on and the outline of a shrimper grabbing a bucket of oil to feed his thirsty engine appeared like a TV set switched on. Not good, Daddy said. Not good.

I stood on the back deck ready to hold or grab anything in case a game warden walked out of the darkness and ruined our whole plan, but the wind just played through the rigging, blowing our high-strung net like a woman's scarf loose from her neck. But not for long, because that high-strung net was the first thing Daddy told me to let down. Next we spent a good half hour straightening out the net seams, flipping webbing this way and that, then doing it again to make sure when he finally threw the net over that he wouldn't throw a twisted net. No sadder fool existed on the bay than a captain who drug for two hours in a good mess of shrimp with an upside-down net. Not only did you get nothing for your trouble, but you'd have the mother of all messes on the back deck, with half the fleet watching while you spent the rest of the day untwisting a pile of wet webbing and mud and hardheads and mashed shrimp. Forget trying to play catch-up.

After the net chore and checking the water and oil levels, then untying a couple ropes and neatly arranging the egg sandwiches and coffee around the wheel in the cabin, Daddy backed the boat stern first into the current, wheeled it around to face the moon, then followed a dozen old license plates nailed on a stick and stuffed into the bay like thermometers in a turkey. The moon flashed off the license plates saying, This way, this way. It was better than a blinking neon light.

Daddy's instinct on the water was gut level and went a hundred miles an hour. Faster than the boat's engine. Faster than the wrecks and submerged pilings and oyster reefs and other shrimp boats that were fifty feet off every point on his bow. We hurtled into the black hole of night, one step ahead of a catastrophe, one plank away from sinking. Yet I stood as easily on the back deck as I stood on the porch at home. It was a confounding, unruly thrust into Nothingness. The fluff of magical thinking. The stuff of dreams. Once when I was four, an uncle who was always joking and pretending he was putting grasshoppers down his throat and cow patties on his head and Spanish moss around his ears like the Swamp Man from the Guadalupe River put me on his feet and lifted me high in the air, yelling, "I'm takin' you to the moon, Silver! I'm takin' you to the moon!" I still remember the terrible thrill of soaring through millions of miles of black space, the moon glowing, the stars flickering and barely missing me as I shot past. The moon sucked the breath from my four-year-old lungs. I was overcome, slain in the spirit of the moon, until my uncle dropped me on my butt. Astronauts don't have nothing on me. I went to the moon.

So I stayed out on the back deck, alone with the drum of the engine beneath my feet and the wind howling through my hair while the lights from the docks vanished from sight. Then the stars came out clear and hot and I walked back into the cabin and drank all the coffee before Daddy did. Daddy wasn't a big talker, but ever' once in a while he'd nudge me in the ribs and say, "Hear them birds?" I could hear them all right, even over the roar of the wind coming through the front window and rattling the door behind us. In those early morning hours Daddy let me hold the wheel while he smoked his cigarettes or walked outside to check the wind direction or to see if he could see the lights of another boat because Daddy's favorite spot on the bay was a spot where no other boat was. My favorite spot was at the wheel with the wind in my face and running with the birds.

Daddy was watching and listening for a game warden's

boat because he wasn't headed for the east side of the reef where the smart shrimpers, the good and obedient shrimpers, had already pitched their nets and were dragging, coffee cups in hand, and complaining over the radio about the damn side of the reef they were dragging on and where the hell was that game warden. Nope, Daddy was aligned with lucky devils. Daddy had thrown in his lot with Satan. We were headed for the dredge holes—far far far from the east side of Panther Point. The dredge holes were ugly and mysterious and had been dug by a dredging company in its latest, hottest pursuit. Not oyster shells this time. Maybe next time. This time it was oil and gas. And those sneaky little shrimp, those crafty and ingenious little fellas, loved to play among dredge holes. It was the equivalent of hiding in a cave. So in that one *for instance*, Chief was wrong about Daddy. He hadn't lost all his magical thinking, 'cause thinking like shrimp *was* magic. Same as Chief talking to the dolphins. Daddy just buried his magical ways under the mumbo-jumbo talk of techniques and nets and dragging speed and rigging and how wide do you turn when you turn on a small spot of shrimp.

It was still dark. All the lights on the boat (starboard, port, mast) were turned off. So was the radio. No talky-talky for the Gray Fox (Daddy's alias on the bay). Secret City to the hilt! Then Daddy threw his net over and got comfortable with a bacon and egg sandwich while I sat on the back deck and watched the flickering lights rise up out of the churning water. Then halfway through a drag and barely sunup, Daddy's net slipped into one of the boggiest of the dredge holes (the dragging trick is to keep the net on the edge of the dredge hole) and we gunked up pretty good with stinking oil-well mud and dead oyster shells and loose rotting seaweed and some crab carcasses from last winter's freeze.

Daddy wasn't too upset. Gunked up nets was normal everyday shrimper stuff and if a fisherman got too upset about ol' mugged-up nets then he oughtn't be a shrimper. Put on an apron and be a grocery clerk instead! So he yanked up the net with a rope, tied it off, and ran the boat a little bit with the net behind, skimming the water's surface. The high hope was that the water would wash the oil-field mud out of the webbing and shove the dead oyster shells down to the sack and hopefully not cut up the sack too much. And forget about the shrimp. There wouldn't be any except for maybe two or three giant shrimp. Then he stopped the boat and we did the hardest work we were going to do the rest of the day. We started yanking up the net by hand, inch by inch, slapping the wet muddy webbing against the boat's side and slinging mud everywhere. I was covered in oil-field mud and half-lulled with the sun and boredom. I was pulling slack webbing like I hardly knew what I did when I spotted a shrimper's glove bobbing in the water. "That's a dead fisherman," I said without putting my thinking cap on straight and I pointed out the glove to Daddy, but Daddy told me to shut up with that stuff. It was bad luck, and lucky devils and bad luck don't run together. Not today. They ain't even kin.

I glanced back over at the bobbing glove, but it was gone. Sunk out of sight with the rest of the drowned body. That's what I thought. It was a bad sign for lucky devils and our tricky situation was getting trickier. Daddy knew it, too, because sweat was running down his neck and his head was half cocked to take in the radio that he had turned on again and was now blasting out stories about what all the shrimpers were catching or not catching, lying or not lying about (put a shrimper in the middle of shrimp and watch a liar get born), but most important, was a game warden's skiff zipping around the bay?

There was a sad story getting told on the radio and the telling got convoluted because every shrimper notices something different on a boat so the telling got different ever time it was told. It wasn't lying. Not really. It was just something they do because shrimpers notice things. There was not a new net, a new bolt, a new piece of rigging, or a shiny deck bucket on a boat that didn't get noticed. And a shrimp boat wandering out of shrimp? One that went round and round in circles? It just don't happen. Shrimpers don't wander out of shrimp. Not deliberately anyhow. It's like a man dropping five dollars out of his wallet for the fun of it. Was that man a lunatic? So after the wandering-out-of-the-shrimp captain couldn't be reached on the CB radio, another boat pulled alongside of him and the captain hollered but that didn't do nothing so he boarded the boat and found the shrimper down in the bilge, passed out from carbon monoxide poisoning.

Daddy's boat had a rebuilt gasoline motor and was the fastest thing around (including the game warden's skiff) and everybody knew it (including the game warden). Case closed. So it was a mighty good thing Daddy was listening to the radio that morning because Daddy was asked to haul the comatose shrimper to the docks where an ambulance from the next town was hopefully waiting. We're looking at minutes, Billy! Minutes! That's what he was told.

So one shrimper hauled the body to Daddy and Daddy tucked him against the homemade icebox on the back deck so he could get plenty of fresh air and maybe revive himself and maybe not get jolted around too much. I was told to sit with him. That's what you get for pointing out that floaty in the water, Daddy said. Then he hitched up his motor and the engine whined in protest. Now, Daddy knew every reef in the bay like he knew his own kids' names. Frontward, backward, and in his sleep. But a dying man on the back deck can rattle any man's soul and it must've rattled Daddy's because when he shoved the throttle into high gear and turned the wheel hard to avoid a reef, he slammed his shrimp boat high center on the next oyster reef and threw me and the fisherman over his muddy stinking net and out into the water.

I was floundering in the water, but the shrimper just sunk. The shrimper didn't rise again. The shrimper couldn't. He was stone-cold dead and when his spirit departed, he flew over the muggy wetness of a startled kid and saw a game warden's skiff going in just as he was leaving. I didn't see any of this myself; I was getting it all vicariously from the dead flying shrimper. Eventually, though, I got my thinking cap on straight. That's when I saw the game warden. He was standing in his game warden skiff with his eyeshades on and he said, "Whatcha doin' out there, little honey?"

I wasn't entirely sure. The sun was buzzing around

my head like killer bees murdering honey in a honey-comb. Finally I spit up a little water and said, "Not a dang thang."

"Not a dang thang, huh?" he said. Then he laughed and went, "Not a dang thang, not a dang thang."

TEN

The Bible is full of fishermen. Fishermen sitting with Jesus. Fishermen talking with Jesus. Fishermen running around and making plans and going out on boats with Jesus. Disciples, for Pete's sake! So you'd think it'd help having a whole churchload of fishermen. But nope, the fishermen were smelling like rotten shrimp on a dung-hill in the nostrils of God. A bunch of filthy, deprived, and nasty shrimp lovers, chewing and smoking and snuffing their way to the fish house to unload their dead.

Forget them missionaries. Forget them sisters slain in the spirit (not dead after all). The Church of Jesus Loves You was under attack by the devil because the bay was under attack by the devil (dead fishermen everywhere; three in three months) and he was doing a pretty good job of it.

Brother Beller was hot and heavy on the subject of the Evil One acting up after the last fisherman was brought in under a tarp. What the church needed was a good ol'-fashioned brush arbor revival to kick that devil out! So he was loaned two acres of pin oak trees and dewberry vines outside of town where he and several brothers whacked the tops off four corner trees, macheted everything in the middle, then strung a makeshift tent roof over a dozen benches built from planks pulled off a sunken wharf. Then the word went out on a loudspeaker on the tail end of a truck: A soul harvest for Jesus! Jesus Christ is the same yesterday, today, and forever! Jesus works today the same way he worked in the first century. Jesus did miracles in the first century, so Jesus can do miracles today. Jesus healed the sick, Jesus looked after the poor, so Jesus can heal the sick and look after the poor in the twentieth century. Praise Jesus, Christ is imminent. Praise Jesus, Christ is among the people.

That might interest the Holy Ghost. That might turn the tide.

So Momma made a last-ditch effort to drag Daddy out of the TV room on Sunday night and untie his unwitting ensnarement to tobacco and other sins she could only imagine. What he lost in the Navy, he could get back again. It was all just details anyhow and churches had a million different details between them.

Some used wine at the last supper and some wouldn't touch the stuff—only unfermented grape juice. Some liked foot washing and others said it was a lascivious effort of the devil to distract us with flesh. Some (the Jesus People) refused to say the words *Father, Son,* and *Holy Ghost* because those weren't names. (Even *Christ* wouldn't cut it.) Only Jesus was a name and the Bible said to ask it in Jesus's name. Then there was the Holiness People, who believed in godly holy lives and wouldn't let the Jesus People preach in their church, and the Pentecostal, who spoke in tongues, claiming the Holy Ghost, and believed everybody else was going to hell. Some saw all manner of nature (mountain, rivers, trees, blood, fire, water, light) involved in biblical motifs: blood splattered on a white dress, tongues of fires above the church, angels fluttering about the moon, Holy Ghost oil dripping from the ceiling. Others didn't believe in that and said those that did were crazy as a coon and possessed by demons. Then some (like the Baptist, down the road) believed once saved and in heaven's grace was always saved in heaven's grace, but Brother Beller knew different: saints could backslide. Oh boy, could they backslide, and the Baptists were sure gonna be surprised on Judgment Day.

Aunt Teny was a Baptist, but no matter, she had a car. And every evening at four o'clock, she showed up in a light blue Ford Fairlane with her three kids in the backseat and if we weren't outside playing in the poison oak or shooting homemade arrows at each other when she arrived, we were soon sent outside with the screen doors locked behind us.

Aunt Teny's visit today took a different track. No coffee and gossiping over people's dirty laundry. No talking about how awful men were. No talking about rusty knives and what they'd like to do with them. Momma had decided her evangelizing conversation with Daddy needed to be at the bay and not the house. The house held no sway over Daddy and, in fact, lessened Momma's influence, which wasn't much to begin with. Momma's influence was solidly located in what Daddy called the dumb end of the stick. In other words, watching the kids and cooking meals and washing clothes. So Aunt Teny and Momma and six of us kids piled into her car and headed for the fish house even though Daddy's Chevy car was sitting, untouched and rusting, at the house. Daddy didn't allow nobody in his Chevy because it was stinkin' with fish, he said, and besides Momma didn't drive so well. Anyhow, we rode with Aunt Teny to where the shrimpers were unloading their shrimp and spreading nets to repair in the sun and generally just hanging around. Momma walked over to Daddy, who had already docked his boat and unloaded his shrimp and was carrying his old stinky shrimp clothes in one hand and a bucket of wrinkled crabs that was most all of what he caught in the other. He handed them to Momma before she had a chance to say anything and said, "Fry these up, Goldie," and Momma let out a shriek because she didn't like cleaning live-looking crabs neither.

In the meantime kids scattered in every direction of the wind. I went down to the tide by myself. Typical typical. Seabirds pecked the foam and tormented little crabs, sending them scampering to their wet dugouts. Sometimes the foam came up around my feet and I put my ear to the wave to listen to the Old Seafaring Grandma's complaints. I was soaking my head good on one side when I saw Daddy climbing into his truck all by himself. Then the rest of us kids and Momma and Aunt Teny crowded back into the Ford car. Momma held a deck bucket of live crabs in her lap while I was told to hang my head out the window and try not to get everybody wet.

Surprise surprise. Daddy agreed to nothing. The artillery of hell that was turned loose on him in the Navy was still loose and there was nothing left to save so Momma might as well forget it. God's promise breakers (and he was one) needed to be exposed, judged, and cast off. And while Daddy squeaked up short on the exposure part (more Secret City) he was very gracious about casting himself out of heaven or wherever. He told Momma the best way that the Church of Jesus Loves could keep out foul and hellish spirits was to build big walls and keep folks like him out. Don't accept their money neither.

So Daddy missed the tent revival, but not Momma and me. We were doing double duty, or at least I was, because when Brother Beller asked for an altar call and all the sinners to come home, I answered, "Yes yes, Jesus, I am trying to come home, but I have too many sins." Every sin Daddy harbored, I harbored. The sins of the father were passed to the kids. It was no different from a family member caught stealing. Don't matter that you didn't do it; you were implicated by your blood. So I was leaning outta the light by reason of my Daddy. And there wasn't nothing God couldn't stand worse than somebody leaning in their own light. How was God gonna get his army with everybody leaning out? There was an urgent and weepy prayer service at my chair. "Pleeease dear Lord Jesus, don't let me lean out. Don't let me lean out. Oooh Jesus, oooh Jesus." Then to reel myself closer into heaven I burst into singing, "This little light of mine, I'm gonna let it shine, let it shine let it shine let it shine."

I was sitting by Momma and it was still early yet and nothing was going according to schedule. But Brother Beller said that was a good sign. The Holy Ghost was wandering and moving. He just loved an uncharted religious odyssey. So trust it trust it! Didn't y'all know the Holy Ghost dictated the whole Bible? Yes, he did, and the Holy Ghost knows what he's doing. So don't worry about that doctrinal doodoo that says you gotta do this first and gotta do that next. Nooo, folks. I say to all those scribes, Pharisees, and heresy hunters out there who condemn us Holy Rollers for holding a knock-down and drag-out service to get out of God's way. Quit blocking God's bridge. God's gonna shoot you down if you don't. He don't wanna see your ugly face.

Sister Pearl was at the piano and pounding out "Shall We Gather at the River?" Two sisters on the front row practiced a gospel song written on a kid's notebook paper. They harmonized a high note, backed off, and then hummed the rest. They were waiting on the Holy Ghost. Nobody was moving but the Holy Ghost didn't move them first. If the sister sitting in the front row wanted to sing one song but the Holy Ghost wanted her to sing two, then she better be prepared to sing two songs. If a brother in the back was a bit shy and didn't like talking much, but the HG wanted him to get up and shout how Jesus's blood had comforted him in a time of great despair, then he better do it. And if it ended up a long drawn-out sermon, well, so be it. Just so long as he didn't drown out the preacher when the preacher told him it was time to wind down.

So one old grandma stood up and said the Holy Ghost was weighing heavy on her heart, telling her to ask for prayer because her backslidden children who had been brought up in the Lord were driving her to distraction. Just see here how she had to hold on to the front chair to keep from falling over. Yes, Lord, she needed prayer, but she also wanted to testify how the Lord Jesus had healed a bad toe she had hit with a shovel last week.

So testifying was next. Normally anybody who needed prayer or healing or just plain wanted to praise Jesus for His Sweet Abiding Arms was welcome to get up and talk without a stopwatch being punched. Sisters, brothers, little kids, delinquent teenagers, drunks, strangers off the street! Jesus was an equal-opportunity savior. Get up and testify what Jesus has done.

The next testifier was a young white-haired stranger. He was shaved but not shaved good. He said he was a hay bailer (out in the sun and rolling in the hay). Then he graduated to a shrimp boat where he got shrimp poisoning in his hand. Then he tried to drink himself well from that shrimp poisoning but all that did was land him in jail. So he wanted to testify how he found Jesus in a jail cell.

From an early age he had roamed (he said he didn't have a momma) where he wanted to and when he wanted to and he got white-haired from the misery of tromping all those bayous and marshes from Florida to east Louisiana. His life had been short and violent. So violent, in fact, that while he was in jail he'd been working on killing this fella. Thinking hard on it. That was what was keeping him sane. You know what I mean? Anyhow, he wasn't exactly sure how he was going to kill the fella, but he had smuggled a screwdriver in his shoe and was working out the dullness by rubbing it against the cement floor. Then the guard shoved a bologna sandwich through the bars at him and he was thinking nothing of it. He wasn't hungry. He was fixed on working out the dullness of that screwdriver. So he let the bologna sandwich set for a full forty minutes at least. Maybe more. Then he picked it up and something unbidden, unexpected, and alarming happened with that ordinary piece of white bread.

Actually it was TWO ordinary pieces of white bread with a thin greasy slice of bologna stuck between them and

that's pretty much the meal in a jail cell. Bologna sandwiches. Nothing special. And it ain't unusual for a guard to
show just who is boss by leaving his handprint in the bread.
Or his thumbprint. Even your food ain't your own in a jail
cell. So this one piece of bread had the guard's handprint,
and in the handprint: Jesus's face! There it was: two eyes,
a long thin nose, a straight mouth curved downward like
he just got pulled off a crucifix by a dirty guard who was
fixing to stab him next. It was unmistakable! He called the
jailer. Did the jailer do it on purpose? What was the meaning of this? What was the jailer thinking? Next he believed
he might have worked himself into a crazy lather thinking
about that man he was fixing to kill. That was when Jesus's
eyes in that sandwich struck him down with a bolt of bril-
liant white light that shot straight through the top of his
head and went out his feet. KAPOW. And he went down
on the floor like a sack of wet oysters. He estimated he was
down for hours, his face jerking, his lower teeth clattering with his top teeth. His tongue started to wag and he
couldn't do nothing with it. He couldn't make it stay in his
mouth.

Then, after he didn't know how long, he fell into heavenly trance and went to heaven and he knew it was a heaven
because his body was IN JAIL and that wasn't heaven.

"The Lord lifted this newborn saint into the heavenlies
and from that high are-eea I surveyed the terrible lostness
of the world and I cried at the terrible suffering, saying,
'Oh Lord, why are you showing me this terrible lostness? I
can't do nothing about it. I am a bad bad man. Looky here,
Lord, at this screwdriver. I was fixing to kill a man.'

"But the Lord said, 'You are a new man now and I have a plan for you, Cotton. Now eat this bologna sandwich.' And I said, 'But Jesus, your face is in that sandwich and I don't wanna do it, I wanna keep it. Put it under that mattress there and keep it.' But the Lord said, 'No. I want you to eat this sandwich, Cotton. It is my body and will give you dynamite to slay mine enemies.' And I asked, 'Oh Lord, what is this dynamite?' And the Lord said, 'You wait just a minute, Cotton. I'm gonna show you.'

"Then Jesus put this terrible terrible hunger for that sandwich in my mouth. And I ate it—I didn't want to. I had to eat it—I was ashamed to eat it, yet I had to. I shook so horrible when I ate that sandwich that I had to hold on to the bars in that cell and that made such a terrible racket that the guard came back and he shouted, 'Shut up, you!' But I couldn't. Just like I couldn't keep my tongue in my mouth, I couldn't stop making that terrible racket. So the guard, he come back again, but this time he had a bucket of cold water and he THREW it on me, yelling and cussing, saying, 'See if this don't cool you down some, you SOB!'

"But it didn't, you know. Praise Jesus, it didn't cool me down a drop because the Lord whispered in my ear, 'You're a new man now, Cotton, and I'm gonna call you Brother Dynamite after the dynamite power I've given you. But you know, this will give the devil trouble and the devil is sitting out there, too—wondering what is gonna happen next. So I'm gonna tell him the same time as I tell you. Brother Dynamite, I want you to call that guard back in here again and ask him for a Bible. Then I want you to read Mark 16, verses 17 to 18.'

"Folks, real as I'm standing here tonight, I didn't know nothing about Mark 16. It's been a long long time since I've opened a Bible and, truthfully, I couldn't tell you if Mark was in the front of the Bible or the back of the Bible, so after I asked that guard for a Bible, and praise Jesus, he brought it, I asked the Lord, 'Where is chapter Mark, oh Lord?' And the Lord said, 'Trust me, Brother Dynamite.' So I trusted on the Lord and flipped opened the Bible and it opened exactly on Mark 16.

"This is what I read: 'And these signs shall follow them that believe; In my name shall they cast out devils, they shall speak with new tongues; They shall take up serpents; and if they drink any deadly thing, it shall not hurt them; they shall lay hands on the sick, and they shall recover.'

"But the Lord warned me! 'Brother Dynamite, I'm giving you the most dangerous gift of all: the handling of snakes. It's as dangerous as dynamite but it won't harm you. Not if you're fully anointed by the Holy Ghost. So you better be fully anointed before you stick your hand in that snake's mouth!'"

He danced a few steps, saying, "Thank you, Lord! Thank you, Lord! I understand now. I understand, precious Jesus."

Then he knelt down and pulled a wooden box out from under his chair and he stood again and held the box high over his head. "Brothers and sisters, this here is some snakes. Lots of snakes. I got them out there in the country. Been collecting them since the day I got out of jail. Now, I don't know what y'all are thinking but I'm thinking y'all believe I might just have fixed these snakes so they won't bite. I didn't. But I can put a matchstick behind one these ol' rattler's venom sacks and squeeze it a little and show you the yellow poison coming out of his fangs. If that's what it takes for y'all to believe me then I can do it. I'll show y'all if y'all want. . . . Okay? Is everybody okay? Don't need for proof? Well then, Lord, I'm asking you to remove this fear of snakes in my heart because I know for sure that venom is bad. But if the Lord anoints me to overflowing with the Holy Ghost, then no harm shall come to me. So in Jesus's name I'm asking it. Amen."

Then he lowered the box onto his chair and opened up the lid and grabbed an armload of snakes. There were dark and light snakes, giant and tiny ones. Coiled, extended, knotted together. Rattlers, cottonmouths, corals, and copperheads. He lifted them up and stared at them nose to nose and one crawled out of the pile and wrapped around his neck. A space opened up before him like he was Moses parting the waters with a stick and the stick was a snake and we were the wave and I was the wave, too, but I was a wave heading in. I had turned completely around in my chair anyhow.

Brother Beller was down front now. He had come clean off the pulpit and his shoulders were squared off and his mouth was a little open and his finger was going a mile a minute. "Here now, here now," he was saying.

Snakes were dripping everywhere, coming around Brother Dynamite's back with their tongues flicking flicking, then coming around again and wrapping around his waist and going inside his shirt. One snake was sliding down his pant leg to the floor and another snake was climbing the air when somebody moaned, "Be with him, Jesus. Help him, Jesus."

If the congregation was a wave rolling out before, it rolled back again, bringing outstretched hands like pebbles strewn in the ocean. Some stroked the air around the squirming mass of snakes and some simply rested their hands against the snake handler's back or his arm. One brother reached to grab a black snake that had crawled up Brother Dynamite's head like he was heading for the ceiling but Brother Beller jumped in front of him, yelling, "Brother! I command you to get back! Satan is in this service! Our Father in heaven, rebuke every power of Satan in this room! Bid every demon depart, every oppressing power of Satan! Saints! Brothers and sisters! Do not be taken in by the devil in this man's hands! Oh, Lord my God, we have stirred up the devil furiously. Oh Lord! Oh Lord!"

But Brother Beller was furiously ignored. Because whether Satan or the Holy Ghost, something was playing hot potato with a rattlesnake.

ELEVEN

I wanted to swing in the tire hanging from the tree limb and watch flames shoot out of the sky or at least angels sit in the chinaberry tree with their legs dangling, but Momma yanked me over to where Brother Beller and the deacons were sending the devil packing. They were in a circle, talking quiet, munching crackers and crumbing some around the foundation of the church. Brother Beller hollered, "I declare the body of Christ has sanctified this ground!" Then he passed around a bottle of grape juice and all the deacons took a swig and Brother Beller walked around the cracker line and poured a bloodline of grape juice.

"Now hear us, devil. Your time is ended. The Church of Jesus Loves You is sanctified by the Holy Body of Christ and no devil shall enter here. We command you to go now, in the name of JEEESUSSS!"

Brother Beller said it was the Holy Ghost who had alerted him first to the devil's presence, so when he pitched that snake-handling devil out—and he had no doubt that he didn't—it was thanks to the Holy Ghost.

Brother Tom was a tall skinny deacon with a big watch latched to his pocket that he took out all the time, especially when he passed the collection plate on Sunday morning, and he did it again like he was checking the amount of time the devil was gone. Then he repocketed the watch and leaned into Brother Beller's ear and whispered, "Brother

Beller, that devil sure carried a big load of admirers out with him. Where you think they were headin' with those snakes?"

Brother Beller snorted, "Brother Tom! I don't care where they were heading! They can head to the moon for all I care. I just know this church nearly fell into a satanic setup! And I ain't positively sure we are clear yet. But what IS crystal clear to me is WHO is building the gallows. The devil! That crazy fella will do anything—be it water moccasin, rattlesnake, or woolly mammoth—to get saints off track and off the word of God! And he did his dead-level best now, didn't he, Brother Tom? Can't say the devil doesn't try. That's the story we need to tell our babies around our knees."

He was looking over at Momma now. "Ain't it, Sister Goldie? Can't say the devil doesn't try. And all this foolishness? Well, don't tempt the Lord with foolishness. Snakes or whatever . . . all this foolishness. Personally, I fear that poor fool will try to drink battery acid next. Ponder *on that* if you will. You can't snooker the devil! You'll just get snookered yourself! Dynamite power! That wasn't dynamite in that poor boy! That was just a pathetic pursuit of the devil. As Paul said, 'All do not work miracles.'"

Me and Momma rode home with Sister Pearl, who was pretty mum about the whole snake deal, not saying yea or nay, not saying if she was going home to wash a snake-handling preacher's shirt and britches for his next demonstration. It was an odd moment of quiet for Sister Pearl. Momma's feelings were crystal clear, though, because two deep canyons formed in the middle of her eyebrows and she looked exactly like she did when she was burning deer meat in a skillet and ruining a perfectly good meal. Conflict did not set easy with her.

I was getting myself a gigantic bellyache—feeling just like a kid who was told by her favorite and most trusted teacher that flying saucers were real. And not only real, they were landing right outside of her bedroom window! Just stick your head out there and take a gander at that! I couldn't wait to go home and tell Sheena that boys weren't the only dangerous things to kiss on the lips.

The only one unimpressed was Grandma. She came from a long line of Holiness preachers (some in Arkansas and some in Oklahoma and one in Texas) and minor miracles and strange goings-on happened to her all the time. "Child," she said, "I will tell you this. If you find a man that tells you he believes in the Bible and preaches that the Bible is the true and inspired holy word of God . . . but he won't have serpent handling? Whyyy, he's not preaching four-corner-square gospel—the full gospel of Jesus Christ the Savior, the Sanctifier, the Healer, and the Coming King. Either all of the Bible is true or none of it is true. Viper handling is just the hardest gift of the Holy Ghost is all. Raising the dead is the other one. What that snake-handling preacher was saying, whether Brother Beller was listening or not, was that we can't always just get the parts of the Bible that make us comfortable. Brother Beller might want a tame Bible so he can sleep good at night! Well, child, the Bible cannot be tamed! So let that Brother Beller and his ilk practice what suits them all they want, but see how far that gets them when hell's flames is licking their feet on Judgment Day."

BROTHER Dynamite put up a sign in a rattletrap car given to him by an enthused fan and the sign read: THE LAST ENEMY IS DEATH. Underneath was a handwritten open invitation to the NEW JESUS CHURCH WITH SIGNS FOLLOWING. MEETING NIGHTLY. It never said where because where don't matter when gossip moves faster. Anyhow, Brother Dynamite drove around in his borrowed car with his sign and ever' now and then he stopped in the middle of the road or pulled off into the ditch and gave everybody that come by a little treat of what was to come at the nightly church service. Usually it was just a guitar treat where he sat on the car's hood and strummed three strings from a five-string guitar. (The full-snake regalia was saved for the old dumping-ground road where under a large mott of mesquite trees and in an area roped off to keep out the unannointed, Brother Dynamite performed his dangerous viper handling.) After thirty minutes or so of guitar picking he'd get back in his car again and in between the windows his head and the old blond guitar looked like a family of Florida towheads. A big one and a little one. Then he'd drive on down the road and do it all over again. Sometimes he'd run out of gas and then he'd just wait until someone come along and filled his tank. The sheriff had already been called in but like the double murder, the sheriff did nothing. Wasn't against the law, he said. Religious freedom or some such thing he didn't explain. He didn't explain himself a whole lot.

Then, and whether it was because he was a snake-handling enthusiast or he just wanted to get Brother Dynamite out of town, a local fisherman loaned him a run-down shack on the Guadalupe River where he could handle snakes all he wanted and others too, if they wanted.

The two-room river shack was plenty big for Brother Dynamite. He didn't have much except an old mattress he drug out of a Goodwill box and the screwdriver he kept to remind himself of his past and the snake box and the blond guitar he kept to remind himself of the future. Then too Sister Pearl gave him a pair of dark pants and two white shirts and told him there was more where that come from if he didn't mind clothes that folks had thrown out. No, ma'am, he said. One pair of pants was fine with him. Then he lined everything up in a straight row on a dusty shelf. His whole life on one shelf. Which was just fine with him; he wasn't attached to anything more than riding around in his car and advertising Jesus and the snake faith that cured all evil. That was his bottom line.

The shack had a working door except the hinge on the bottom was gone and saints that came to his church had to lift the door a little and yank the door open. Then underneath the oak trees he found a chair with four legs weakened by oak leaves and the sweet rot that came from the river running so close by and he drug that in too. Then a brother who had left Brother Beller's church that first night and appointed himself deacon of the New Jesus Church with Signs Following went to the garbage dump outside of town and drug back a busted shrimp door that they turned upside down with the chains rusting and dragging on the

floor and pounded four boards for legs. They had a pulpit
and they were open for Jesus business.

The church wasn't easy to find. Only real river rats
(commercial fishermen who worked on the river) knew
the exact whereabouts because the shack was the former
hidey-hole of the outlaw hunter/fisherman that loaned it
to Brother Dynamite and was purposefully built to disappear behind green twisting vines and elephant ears and
willow trees dripping so low in the river that the catfish
living there thought they were home. So ever' time a snake
enthusiast visited, he had to get clear directions on getting
back home.

At first there weren't many takers. The crew that had
wandered out with him that first night had second thoughts.
But by the fourth night they were back, and a few more
besides. Some just waited on the sidelines. Waiting on the
snakes. That was all they were there for. They were the
same sort that went to the carnival and visited the lady with
warts all over her head. They stood (they didn't bother with
sitting) in back with arms folded and if Brother Dynamite
was slow about anointing himself or if a snake was particularly mild (sometimes a snake pulled out of the box hung
like a wet noodle caught in the middle) he was accused
of putting them to sleep with hypnosis, dosing them with
liquor, handling them too much, exercising them at night
to wear them out, or feeding them too much. No snake
with a bellyful of rats will strike! Once a snake died after the
nightly handling and a man hollered through the window
that he'd find a snake that would bite that sucker! And he
was going to get it. Then he left and when he returned,

he threw some elephant ears through the window and hollered, "Snake, snake!"

Brother Dynamite said the devil (the snake) was tempting that man to bring in something besides elephant ears to throw in a window. Don't matter. The Lord told him— Brother Dynamite, standing right here—that he could handle anything anybody brought in. Just bring it in. He wanted them to. He wasn't a bit worried.

"If the Lord wants me to ride an alligator, whyyy, I'll do that, too! If you have faith, you won't get harmed. But if you do get bit it's because the devil stole you away from God. And you let 'em. You lost your faith. And when I say *faith* I mean getting rid of planning and preparation and money money money. If you're gonna follow Jesus, just go. Jesus calls and you go; you don't hesitate. You don't need training, you don't need the church's backing, you don't need the town's backing. Jesus is gonna provide for you."

He said he could preach snake handling out of any book of the Bible too, and to prove it he put the Bible across the busted shrimp door, laid a snake alongside it, and flipped open the Bible. Jeremiah, Isaiah, Amos, Zechariah. Luke 10, verse 19: "Behold, I give unto you power to tread on serpents and scorpions, and over all the power of the enemy: and nothing shall by any means hurt you." Acts 28:3–6: Paul shook off a viper that was fastened on his hand without suffering any ill effects. Exodus 4:2–4: Moses, at God's command, transformed his rod into a serpent and picked it up by the tail.

"Folks, there is a difference between being religious and being spirit filled. If I was just religious I'd still be sitting there in that Church of Jesus Loves You. And welcome too, probably. More welcome than I am now. Now, I'd be run off on a fence post like I almost was last time. But I'm spirit filled, anointed by the Holy Ghost, and, folks, that is like swallowing God. It flows from your head to your toes. It is God liquidized. Like drinking red sodie water. Only better. Much much better. And folks, anybody can drink! Even people that don't have any digestion or their gut is eaten up with ulcers. Got a cancer in their bellies. Drink up, folks. It is an aid to digestion. The cracked lightning of firsthand experience. Learned from the inside out and not driven in with a sledge hammer from the outside in."

THE second week of snake handling in the run-down river church jump-started a week of revival at the Church of Jesus Loves You and by curious coincidence too it bumped up the arrival of Aunt Silver and her two kids—twins, a boy and a girl—and her preacher husband from Idaho. It was a big surprise to everybody. She hadn't called or wrote anybody, probably thinking (knowing!) her sisters would have told her to stay in Idaho since she liked it so much. She went there, married there. So stay in Idaho. They'd take care of what was in Texas (that was Grandma, who was giving away all her shrimp checks to that fornicating evangelist).

But kinfolks are kinfolks. And they are fed no matter what and first thing too. So one of my brothers who pitched fastballs at a baseball field and wore purple socks up to his pants legs shot and butchered a deer, and everybody else (except me and Aunt Silver's girl twin, who stayed at my Uncle Dutch and his redheaded wife's house, where a little tree sat on a coffee table and the wife trimmed it with fingernail clippers) went "cooning" oysters with Daddy on his boat because above all else—and practically next to Jesus!—Aunt Silver loved oysters. She couldn't get enough of oysters! After living all those years in cold cold Idaho and eating nothing but frozen potatoes for breakfast, dinner, and supper she couldn't get enough oysters. Aunt Silver said even if Doomsday came (and by her calculation it was somewhere in the near near future) it wouldn't be around suppertime tonight cause Jesus wouldn't waste perfectly good fried oysters. Jesus loved fried oysters too!

So Momma fried deer meat and oysters dunked in corn-meal until black smoke billowed from the skillet and out the kitchen door and ruined the big sunny living room with the mirror and the couch and the black Bible lying on a coffee table. Then she did it again the next day because Aunt Silver's love of oysters knew no bounds.

Aunt Silver was a youth minister (the only REAL convert out of four girls and four boys) and in her younger days she could walk on her hands and beat ever' boy around. But for the last twelve years she had hoed taters in the cold cold fields of Idaho where she and her Idaho preaching husband and two kids lived. Now she was back in Texas where she would stand with Jesus and Grandma.

She also was a mass of contradictions. Her water side wanted to fly God's colors into the battlefield of Good and Evil, shooting enemies of the cross with a Holy Ghost machine gun while radiating waves of holiness and influencing everybody around (particularly in Idaho, where her holiness floated upon Idaho's airwaves awaiting her return). Her vinegar side, however, would wear the hide off a fence post. So when her sisters (so surprised that she arrived back in Texas again) said, "Changing your tune so fast are you, Silly Silver?" Aunt Silver said she wasn't changing her tune at all. No, ma'am! And then she argued the hide off a fence post denying it. (Aunt Silver had enormous staying power and won won won every argument.)

But Aunt Silver was getting the devil in church because the Church of Jesus Loves You, particularly Brother Beller, didn't allow women to do nothing that men could do first. No women authority over the men. That included preaching. It couldn't be emphasized enough, Brother Beller said, that women were to be good, submissive, discreet, chaste, silent (if you want to learn something or ask a question in church, ask your husband at home so you won't disrupt the service), homemakers not slanderers, not given to wine (just grape juice), teachers of all good things, loving to their children, obedient to their husbands (support his ministry!), helpers of the poor, doers of good works, mothers to all in the church. And yes yes, the Bible did show some clear examples of women teaching, but it was older women teaching younger women and children. And while there were a few examples of women in leadership roles over men (for instance, Deborah) this was the exception. Not the norm; not the rule.

That attitude was exactly why Aunt Silver was in children's church and not adult ministry. Adult ministry was flat-out unwomanly. Didn't matter to Aunt Silver. There was more than one way to skin that church cat. So while her husband pastored in Idaho, of course she did too. She stood in front of the church (a short short woman, wide as she was tall, with loosened hair longer than she was tall but always up on her head in a doughnut that bounced out the pins as the day wore on), telling a Bible story to the children sitting in the front two rows with their feet barely scraping the floor. But the storytelling got so involved, got so physical, that she eventually wiggled her way into evangelizing to the parents sitting in the back rows. They certainly got the message too. Same as the front row.

Aunt Silver was so involved in winning over the church that at first she didn't realize that there was a race going on between the river church with its busted-shrimp-door pulpit and madman occupant and the Church of Jesus Loves You. She had arrived a day too late to hear Brother Beller in his sermon one night call Brother Dynamite a self-exalting madman leading God's sheep astray. Whyyy, those poor starved bleating sheep were probably eating the wool off each other! But Brother Beller believed he was gonna win that tug-a-war for the sheep. So some teenagers got resaved, a couple brothers rededicated their lives, and a drunken deckhand wandered in from the street and was saved too. But two weeks of steady revival preaching was wearing him down and that's the real reason Aunt Silver was invited to do a children's church service on Sunday NIGHT! Glory of glories! Sunday night! Sunday-night preaching was only for men but Brother Beller was making a special exception to the rule. Besides, Momma and her

brood of kids were long-standing members and who knows
how many kinfolks Aunt Silver could bring in. His thinking was right on the button because Aunt Silver invited
the entire family even though Momma was the only good
Pentecostal left. (Aunt Teny and Aunt June Bug wore
golden hoop earrings, and Uncle Dutch's redheaded wife
smoked cigarettes! And dyed her hair red.) Plus Grandma.
That would have been a major victory! It had been years
since she had stepped foot in the church. But Grandma
wasn't coming no matter what, no matter how hard Aunt
Silver cajoled, then soothed, then pried, until Grandma was
a seething pile of fury and turned her radio on full blast.

So it was an extra-special family night with Sister Silver
officiating and the Mullins girls (Momma and all her sisters)
the main focus, so Aunt Silver wanted us all to sit together.
Show off what a big family in Christ we all were. I was praying Momma wouldn't sing. Please please, dear Jesus, don't
let Momma sing. There was nothing more embarrassing
than Momma singing. But forget it, Aunt Silver got Momma
to get up and sing a song about an old gray-haired momma
dying and how bad all her kids were. Then too, Aunt Silver,
who was out in the front row and big as Dallas, started praying, Praise God, praise God, praise God, louder and faster,
faster and louder; then all of a sudden she started arching
for the ceiling, but before she hit the rafters words poured
out of her mouth. Aunt Silver was speaking in tongues.
Shamba la leeee lalebe lakadoma mama maa shablalililili
laaaa leeeemakakadonadoneeee. The church got quiet and
the guitarists and fiddlers held their instruments in their
laps. Everybody was waiting on an interpretation for Aunt

Silver's tongue speaking. Then the waiting got too long so Aunt Silver walked the razor's edge of biblical taboos that said God created the temperaments of men and women different just so they wouldn't do what she was fixing to do: interpret her own message. But Aunt Silver didn't worry. She was Pentecostal, and Pentecostals had faith and faith was the absence of planning.

Aunt Silver shouted, "The working-class folks will soon rest from their hard labor and their daily struggle to keep their lives pure in a world full of sin. It is all coming to an end very soon and ye little worms of dust sitting in the church will soon be transformed in a twinkling of the eye into glory and immortality."

It sounded good to everybody. Hallelujah and praise Jesus. This old weary world was fixing to end! Then on the crest of her last hallelujah, Aunt Silver moved into her Bible story for the children, which was about old evil King Nebuchadnezzar throwing God's faithful servants Shadrach, Meshach, and Abednego into the fiery furnace because they wouldn't bow down to the golden god. But the angels arrived in the nick of time and surrounded them with their heavenly white wings and delivered them from the devil's fiery flames. Hallelujah, wasn't that story wonderful? Aunt Silver wanted everybody to listen good because there were serious woes out there. Troubles aplenty in life's fiery furnace. But God sends angels to help us and they arrive just in the nick of time. Oooh, brothers and sisters, there are angels. Shame on us for not believing there are angels. Shame on us.

TWELVE

Jesus came through my dream doorway and said Chief was in for some bad news, and the next morning Chief came through the real doorway, saying, Bad news bad news, Billy. My fishing skiff's done blowed up.

So Daddy took a short ride down to the bay to see what all was left of Chief's skiff, and what all was left of Chief's skiff was a burnt-out hull listing sideways in the mud. Chief said he'd tried to make coffee on the boat that morning on his two-burner kerosene stove but the thang flooded so he threw it overboard and drove into town in Archie's old truck to get a new stove and that's when the boat blew up.

"All on its own," Chief said. "Now, *ain't that* a coincidence."

Daddy said he wasn't going there. Nope. Wasn't doing it. If he wanted to believe shootings and boat burnings were a pile of coincidences, then he could. It was a free country. He could believe what he wanted to believe. Besides, he said, wasn't that skiff supposed to be out yonder in his pasture?

"Well," Chief said, "how you think Archie Don got brung in? Your little baby brother. Brung himself in? Hell, nope. He was brung in on that skiff! I done it. Me! An old man folks seem like they'd rather see sitting on a porch. Folding his hands. Shoot a mile, they can all go to hell."

Daddy said the biggest surprise of all was that Chief didn't get blowed up, too. After all, every shrimp boat, oyster boat, and fishing skiff in the harbor had a gasoline engine and, nine times out of ten, that engine malfunctioned and sent gasoline hither and thither, dancing a jig on the engine, dancing a jig in the bilge, and dancing a jig wherever. So any fisherman stupid enough to go below in a cabin smelling of gasoline and rotten quilts and then light up a Camel or Winston cigarette while doing it deserved to get blown fifty feet across the harbor and into yesterday. Besides, how many stones out there in that graveyard could read BLOWN UP BY A GASOLINE ENGINE if the kinfolks of them that died hadn't been too embarrassed about doing it? How many, you think?

"Listen here, Billy Bonehead. Wasn't no gasoline in that stove. Kerosene was what was in that stove—and it's overboard! Go lookin' for it. Dig it outta the mud. See if you smell gasoline. Nope, kerosene! Kerosene! Oooh, bull crap."

Chief said he was going back to his house. He hadn't been there since he seen Archie as a little black vapor and he'd probably have a hard time contacting him now. Archie Don liked that boat. And it was a pretty-known fact that you need to stay where the spirits visit. Same as that spirit in the Pentecostal church. Now, ain't that right, Billy?

Daddy didn't answer.

Oh yeah. You don't go there no more, Chief said.

Anyhow, to Chief's way of seeing things, the skiff and Archie's ghost were blown up on the exact same day and it was as deliberate as the other one-two shoot-out.

Daddy said, You think that game warden wants more attention drawn his way? *More?* Wants to be accused of blowing up your boat now? That's what you think?

Nope, he don't care, Chief said. He's too far gone around the bend. Besides, he knows he ain't gettin' caught unless I find that gun. Fishing pole too. But mainly that gun. But that boat blowed up. Yep, that boat blowed up. Ruined my communicating with Arch.

Then Chief said he was feeling a little crazy. Maybe he would go lay down a little while in his house. Fold his hands over his belly.

YOU know how it is, Chief told me later. You can't rush into something the game warden knows about before you do it because then the game warden would be standing there with another match to blow up another something. Maybe Archie Don's truck with me in it the next time. Better to let the game warden think he had quit. A burned-out ol' man.

So that's why Chief came over to my window again, knowing how I slept in the window, knowing how easy I was to convince of anything, saying, Hey, girlie, hey, girlie. And I'd roll out to anything. I rolled over to the window screen and Chief said, Go get Patty. Patty's got a boat and if she don't, she'll get a boat. Patty hates game wardens. Her ex-husband and her both had a run-in with that game warden. So she don't have much use for him. Or them. The whole kit and caboodle of them. Send them all back to Austin! Patty carried bad grudges too. That ex-husband refused to do something she wanted—and who knows what it was—and when he died, she buried him backward in his grave. Put his head where his feet were supposed to be!

Anyhow, Chief told me to tell Patty to get a skiff even if she had to buy one. He'd pay for it. He had the broke-off handle of LaSalle's sword that he found out on an oyster reef in the bay and he'd use that for a horse trade. Worth lots of money, that ol' explorer stuff. Patty liked old stuff. Confederate buttons and belt buckles. Horseshoes. Square nails. Heck, she'd love that Frenchy thing. Lots of folks claimed they found something LaSalle lost in the bay that time he ended up in Matagorda Bay when he was heading someplace else. But he had the real thing. Forget them other liars.

Patty lived in a little homemade camper at the turning-off spot to the cemetery road. Nobody visited, not even folks new to town and ignorant as all get-out. Not even if somebody said, Whyyy, why don't you folks go by and meet Patty? 'Cause you'll never have the chance again. There's nobody in the world like Patty and won't be anyone like her again.

Meeting Patty was the biggest dare in town. Some big boys would run to her door, spit, then run like the devil. So when I knocked on the door and Patty hollered out, "Why don't you come on in? You know how to come in, don't you?" I opened the door but knocked all the oyster dust off my feet. Chief already said Patty didn't cotton to nothing. Anything would tick her off. That's when all the dogs came yelping out and I saw three little ol' dogs were still in there. Patty said they were puppies of one of them big dogs. One's name was Beans and the other two were Biscuit and Gravy. It was a pretty bad mess inside with clothes hung over the ceiling joists and dangling over an old black cooking stove that had one leg gone.

I trailed my way through all that mess and Patty said to sit on a cot. The puppies tried to rear up on my legs but Patty hollered at them to get out of the way and lobbed a stick of stove wood toward them and knocked down two and they ran over and jumped up on the cot and looked around like their feelings were kind of hurt. I looked over at Patty and it was getting dark and I hadn't said anything about the skiff yet so I said real quick, "Misses Patty, Chief is sure in a big hurry. . . ."

"Hell, I ain't no misses anymore. Who the hell tole you that? Besides, and hellfire, honey, it's just about suppertime now, so why don't ya stay and eat?"

I said, No no no, I couldn't. I just couldn't do it. . . . No no. And Patty said, "Aw hell, come on in and eat. I'd feel real bad if you don't." Finally I ate something—the red beans, the corn bread, and she had a jar of honey with a little honeycomb floating around in it like a dead jellyfish. I ate that too.

After supper came the skiff question and Patty looked fit to be tied over something. I thought it was something— maybe a fly in her tea glass because she was looking in her tea glass. But it wasn't. It was just game wardens she hated.

Know why? she said. And I said, Ma'am? And she said, Hellfire, you know why?

It was that Ira. That game warden fella. She was out there shrimping in the east part of Matagorda Bay and Ira and this other officer come up and Ira yelled at her to stop the boat and she told him if she stopped now the net was gonna settle on top of the oyster reef and tear the whole bottom up. So Ira climbed on board and kept telling her very loudly to pick up immediately and stop the vessel and he began to shove and push her. He even shoved her sixteen-year-old deckhand who hadn't said a word to him at'all. Then when she told him to not touch her deckhand, Ira told her, I'm gonna blow you away, lady. So she got to thinking she better get in the cabin and try callin' that marine operator to get ahold of a constable in Matagorda. She couldn't believe this was happening and she damn well wanted to get more people involved than just him and her and a little sixteen-year-old kid.

So she went inside and told Ira not to come into her cabin but Ira come anyhow. And by that time the other officer had come on board too and they began discussing who was gonna operate her boat and she told them like she knew it was: it's against the law for anyone to master a vessel except the captain. Well, when she told him that, Ira just said, Well, I can, and he reached for the controls. She told him to get away because she was still handling this boat, and besides, there were too many boats shrimping nearby and any one of those boats might end up ramming someone. So Ira got mad at this and grabbed her shoulder, tearing her shirt and scratching her back. So she reached over and stopped the engine and as she turned around, Ira hit her on the forehead with his fist. At this, she turned around and really didn't know what to do with him, him being an officer and all, so she just tried grabbing him and as she did this, he hit her on the other side of the head. So she just ended up holding on to his legs and put him on the floor so he couldn't hit her. So there they say she assaulted a police officer and she guessed that game warden was what they were calling a police officer, but really all she was doing was just trying to keep him from hitting her.

"So you see, honey? I ain't disagreeing with you and your ol' grandpa a bit. But can Chief handle that game warden? 'Cause that Ira is one mean sunavabitch. A little crazier than most and he don't mind hitting women so he sure don't mind hitting an old man."

On any given day of the week, Patty was dressed in her shrimping outfit: a man's blue jeans, a man's undershirt, and over the undershirt a man's flannel shirt and a man's hat on her head. Her hair was cut short. Everybody in town knew the hat belonged to her late dead husband buried backward in his grave. But the shoes weren't his. They were high, black rubber boots and looked like they'd drown her if she ever fell overboard.

Nobody dared mention the man clothes to her face. If they did she punched them hard on the shoulder or else gave them a fierce glare, saying she could look any way she dammed well wanted to look. After all, you work in the bilge of a boat, you're gonna look like a grease monkey. No need for high fancy looks down there. Mud and grease and an occasional dead crab is all that's looking at you. I'm telling you, it ain't heaven working down there.

Patty didn't have a deckhand anymore because deckhands were usually male and Patty didn't want a male anything on her boat. Next thing you know they were holding the wheel and givin' her orders. And Patty didn't take orders. Best way of working with Patty was to give her the general idea and leave her the hell alone. And if a boat was involved, let her hold the wheel.

Chief said, Okay okay, Patty can hold the wheel. What else did she say?

She said to meet her at the wharf.

In plain sight?

Nooo, I said. When it's dark. Two in the morning. Or midnight. I forgot which. To be on the safe side, we left at midnight. Chief came to the house and I rolled out of the screened window. I was ready for him this time and had on my shrimping clothes and almost looked like Patty. Then we crossed what was left of the backyard and took a short-cut through some shinnery and moonlight, and when we come out into a clearing with the harbor right in front of us, Chief looked like forty years had been erased from his face. When he squinted at the moon he looked young as me.

Patty had a skiff and a tarp and a rope for I don't know what, tying or covering something. Patty said she stole the skiff. Stole the trailer too, to get the skiff. That was how Patty worked—going backward when frontward won't work—and if Chief didn't like it he could just scram, but Chief said he didn't care. He just wanted the boat for this one night. She could take it back later. What man would miss a boat and trailer for one night?

We were halfway across the bay, with the moon just a little slip of a girl, when we planned the whole thing. Patty said normally she didn't plan and she came from a whole line of nonplanners so what she was doing was only on account of that game warden she hated so much. Then Patty quit talk-

Three little angels. (L-R) Shenna, Pill, Silver.

Captain Billy's boat, later sunk somewhere in Matagorda Bay.

Chief in San Antonio Bay.

LEFT: Archie Don with an infant.

BELOW: Silver's alter ego, Anthony Perkins. PHOTO COURTESY MPTV.NET.

TOP: Seadrift Harbor.

LEFT: Brother Billy at a revival.

Facing page
TOP: Family portrait. Silver, Shenna, Billy, Pill, Goldie, Froggie.

BOTTOM LEFT: Pirate Billy Bones.

BOTTOM RIGHT: Aunt Teny with Wayne, Silver, Shenna, Pill.

eadrift hunters. Chief is second from the right.

Grandma Rosa Belle babysitting grandkids.

Silver with short hair.

Grandma Rosa Belle with Wayne and Silver.

ing about the game warden and took a turn at the wheel, then a turn with the quart jar of homemade grape wine, which (we found out) was something else Patty brought besides the rope and only once did she mistake the wave for the wind.

A finger of reefs, mostly dead and bone white, shone in the moonlight. If the tide was higher and the moon a little brighter we could have revved up the motor and skimmed right over the reefs. But it wasn't high tide so we just plodded around and headed for the next bay. Mesquite Bay. Daddy's dream bay of two-thousand-pounds-of-shrimp-a-drag. I'd done the ride a hundred times with Daddy on the shrimp boat so I knew it took a long time. Several hours. I suppose that was why Patty wanted to leave so early. Wasn't nothing like showing up at full bright sunup and showing yourself off to Ira and his little cache of guns. Anyhow, Chief was sure hoping he'd find guns.

It was a good ride across the bay and a light wind, too, so we were guessing (guesswork was a lot of the thinking on the bay and went into every plan) the engine wouldn't suck up all the gas on the way over and leave us stranded with nothing to get back on. Chief said the wind would be at our back on the way back so he guessed we'd make it. Don't worry about nothin', girlie.

An hour and a half later, we pulled up to the island and oyster shells were the brightest things around. White white white like the bay had opened its mouth and showed all its teeth. Next was a whole lotta brush. I couldn't see the game warden's shack, but Patty said we wouldn't see the shack. That's why the shack was there, dummy. Nobody to eyeball it, you *comprendo*?

Patty stopped the boat motor near the reef and we coasted awhile until we bumped the mud bottom. Then Chief started to climb out and Patty said, Now, hell, just wait a minute, Chief, hold on hold on, let me pole a little closer. But Chief was already over the side. The water was shimmering around his boots but not going over the boots' edge, so I climbed out too and the water came up cool around my legs. I looked around. Thick, head-tall shrub covered the entire island. A tourist would've been mighty disappointed. Where's the sandy beach? Where's the birds? Where's the pretty shells?

Whadda y'all see? Patty said.

Nothin' but weeds!

Hell, we're here then, Patty said. She was standing in the skiff, holding a wooden pole twice as long as she was tall, and her face looked like a heavy iron lid had been taken off and she was suddenly seeing daylight for the first time. Whatever we were doing (breaking and entering) Patty liked it! Then she took one hand off the pole, leaned down in the skiff, and slung a pair of old rubber boots at me. "Put them boots on, honey. They ain't nothin' to look at but they'll keep your feet from slicing to pieces on them oyster shells before we even get what we come for."

I pulled on the rubber boots one at a time, balancing on one foot while I yanked on the other. They were plenty loose. Which was good. If I fell over in the deep water I wouldn't drown. I could've kicked them off nicely. But now they just tripped me up when I went looking for Chief. He had disappeared into the brush. Then I nearly ran into him while Patty nearly ran into me.

Well, hellfire, girl. Get on up there. Whatcha dragging your feet for? It's up ahead. Get on.

Where's that path? Chief asked.

Ain't no path, least on this side it ain't. Back side's got a path. On this side you just gotta wind your way in there. Through that shrub brush. Never mind those birds. They'll squawk their heads off but they don't bite.

Chief said he knowed that. Ain't telling him nothin'.

But Patty was paying him never-you-mind, still talking talking. Usually now, she said, Ira comes in that back door. I seen him do it a dozen times. So nobody knows he's there. But he's there. Oh boy, is he there. Why you think he catches those shrimpers and all those fishermen with their gill nets so quick in Mesquite Bay? Got him a little hidey-hole is why. Watchin and a-snoopin'. Hell, he's worse than any shrimper ever lived. . . . Besides, going round that back way is gonna cost us another thirty minutes. And I don't care to run into Ira just 'cause you don't wanna get scratched up.

Oooh shut up for half a second, Chief said. I'm going.

Halfway through the brush they decided on another piece of the plan. I needed to be left out on the oyster-shell beach to be a lookout for that game warden. Ain't he coming around that back side? I said.

Hell yep, but he'll cut through that little cut first. . . . See that piling sticking up? Right there. Then he'll cut round back. But first through the cut. You *comprendo*? Gives us about ten minutes to see what we're gonna see. But taking our time too, 'cause Ira ain't here. . . . Iffen he was, you think I'd be here? Hell, nope. So let's don't both rush that door together, Chief. Just looky and see, looky and see if that gun ain't somewhere. We both know he ain't hauling it in his truck. Everybody in tarnation would be seeing it then.

They left and the moon went behind a bank of dark clouds. What wind there was, was gone now. I didn't know if that didn't mean something. Wind coming? Wind going? Shoot! I was only nine years old. What did I know? So I turned to ask Chief but he and Patty had already gone where you make one turn and you disappear like you were never there. So I just stood watching the water, watching the cloud bank and the moon, hearing the rustling of brush and sometimes Chief and Patty's voices and birds too that were run off their nest. The brush was full of them. Bird nests built exactly like sloppy squirrel nests.

Patty said it was pure guesswork how long that game warden had been claiming squatter's rights to the island. But whatever it was, it was off-and-on squatting 'cause he had to have a Texas street address long enough to claim Texas residence and not Florida for that game warden agency. Sure had to keep them happy. And his wife too. Well, maybe not maybe not. Anyhow, Ira showed up on the island just as that last occupant (a gill-net fisherman) loaded up his pots and pans and clothes onto a skiff and left, leaving behind some worn-out gill nets drying on the shell beach and a rain cistern that he'd had built from rocks and oyster shells and mud and used to water his garden so he could horse-trade fresh vegetables with every shrimper that came through the cut. Fresh onions, Swiss chard, collards, turnips, and tomatoes for shrimp and soft-shell crabs. What a steal.

I was looking across the bay. There were no lights. Too far from town. The next-closest town was on the other side of the bay, and boy oh boy, wouldn't that be something if instead of Ira coming from Seadrift, Ira launched his boat from the town across the bay! I was working myself into a nice panic imagining the whole deal. Then I turned toward a finger of land that stuck out midway between the next town and us. Dagger Point. But there was nothing. Good, good. Ain't nothing like breaking into somebody's house to put you into a nice panic.

Ten minutes more and coming out of nowhere, Patty and Chief shuffled from the brush. Chief said it first. "The gun ain't there. He hid it someplace else."

Then he sloshed into the water, shoved the skiff as he went, and climbed in and held the pole. Then Patty climbed in too, and I was stuck on shore in my big rubber boots.

Well, get a move on, Patty said. Shove us out.

Patty sat at the stern and held the starter rope and both of them were watching me like I was the only picture show in town. So I waded out into the water, put both hands on the bow, and shoved. The boat moved a couple inches. Not enough for nothing. Certainly not enough to let an engine propeller turn. We were stuck like flies on sticky paper. But no matter. What was the hurry? Everybody was sitting quiet, all nervousness gone because we were off the island, in a skiff, and already guessing what was ahead (reefs, moon, sleepy dead-headed people) and already forgetting what was behind (dark, run-down game-warden shack).

Suddenly, Patty jumped straight up and shouted, "Hellfire hellfire. It's that got damn game warden!"

We stopped ever'thing. My shoving, their guessing. Ever'thing. A tiny little devil of a moon slid out from behind some clouds and showed a boat coming fast around Dagger Point.

"Who's that?" I said, but I already knew. Who else would be out here at this time of night?

Patty was still standing, still jumping, and shouting, "Shove the boat shove the boat shove the boat!" And ever' time she jumped she pounded the boat a little farther into the mud. Chief was holding Patty's pole and maybe he was starting to regret messing with Ira, but TOO LATE, he had already messed with Ira, and not only Ira but his shack too. So Chief didn't move but his eyes got big and they were wide as the Spanish coins he was always finding on the shore.

"Helllfiiire," Patty said for the upteenth time, and she grabbed the starter rope and yanked twice. The motor hit a high whine and blew a ton of smoke nobody saw, just smelt, then the propeller hit the mud bottom. Hard. The engine clunked to a stop.

"Oooh, honeeey, put yore back to it," she hollered.

I was. Pouring and pushing and straining my arms and filling my rubber boots full of water. Then I leaned too far in (my head was nearly in the water) and my rubber boots (full of water) cemented themselves in the mud and I hit the water face-first. Warm salty water went up my nose and over my shoulders. I looked up startled, and for a second Patty acted like she was fixing to jump overboard and throttle me. Then she switched plans and planted both legs wide apart with a rubber boot on either side of the skiff and started rocking the boat.

Boat rocking works every time if you're not in a big rush and haven't drunk a quart of homemade mustang grape wine. Otherwise, you're just riveting the boat to the mud with some rapid-fire *whompwhompwhomps*. And with a game warden coming around the point! So I turned, stuck my back to the boat, shoved with both legs, and promptly sunk up to my knees in mud—but the skiff gave a little slide. My rubber boots were lost—beyond redemption—to the hell where all bad boots go. So I climbed out of them and hit the water barefoot. The deeper water was slushy with mud and oyster shells, knee-deep in some places, and one old ancient oyster shell raked across my instep with its butchery edge. I could feel the blood gushing and looked up to Patty, but no sympathy there. She was hunched over the motor, yanking on the starter rope like a maniac, and desperately trying to get some life in the engine. Finally the motor hit and threw her backward onto the engine, and the skiff made a hard run back to the island. I lunged for the sides as Patty straightened the rudder and we headed across the open water. I was dangling, half in and half out of the boat and plowing up a bunch of water, when Chief grabbed me by my arm and yanked me into the boat. I fell into a wet heap in the middle of the skiff.

Barefoot, bleeding, and soaked to the gills, I crawled to the bow on my hands and knees and got the wind full in my face. Off to the left about a hundred yards I got some more bad news. A little gray sliver of a skiff ran diagonally at us.

I turned and looked at Patty.

"That got dang game warden!" she yelled. "He's seeen us!"

Chief, sitting in the middle of skiff, said nothing.

"What's he gonna do?" I hollered.

"When he catches us, I'll let ya know," Chief said.

How do you outrun a game warden's skiff? Well, if our stolen skiff was my daddy's shrimp boat, we'd for sure outrun the game warden. But skiff-to-skiff? Depends on the condition of the boat and the engine. Depends on the hull lines—whether the skiff had a little V shape to it or was flat bottomed and would pound the living daylights out of you before you outraced anything. And Patty's stolen skiff? The skiff owner was getting rid of it, so it couldn't be all that fast. If it was fast he wouldn't be selling it. Unless it was rotten. So our skiff was either rotten or slow. One of the two. It was just a matter of time before we found out for sure. I didn't know what to expect. Ira hadn't done nothing to me besides shoot my uncle and pick me up slooow outta the water that time like I was an interesting cat he found that normally he would have drowned. That time my interestingness saved me. Now I didn't know. My luck was running like a bad hand of dominos.

We weren't heading for the docks. Patty said, "Too far and too late for the docks." So I didn't know where we were headed and neither did she. NEW territory for all of us. A land like no other. Maybe oleander and oak and wild persimmon were waiting for us. Maybe heaven. Finally the heart beating inside that frozen-solid kid that I'd become was freed of all laws and I couldn't recognize the sounds coming from her mouth. It might be tongue speaking! Hallelujah, it sounded like holy-rolling tongue speaking to me. Maybe Jesus would save us all.

"Hush," Chief said. "Hush."

THIRTEEN

Momma was in the middle of frying Daddy's entire last drag, which wasn't much since Daddy had been drug off his boat to pick up a banged-up and nearly drowned certain party that was rammed by a certain game warden's skiff.

Patty was the worst. Even with her head bashed in, even when the sheriff came and then left, and nobody for her to yell at except a nurse who kept rearranging her bandages, Patty wouldn't shut up. And the yelling wasn't about anything or anyone in particular. Not the game warden. Not the boat pileup. Not even her ol' dead ex-husband buried backward in his grave. A dog trotting across the street would have been enough to rile her. It was like Chief said in the beginning about Patty but didn't really mean: anything would tick her off. Now, for sure, anything would tick her off. Chief said Patty had her good sense knocked out. That's what the game warden did for her. Killed Archie Don, but Patty got her sense knocked out.

Daddy didn't go visit Patty with her bandaged head. Daddy grabbed me with my bandaged and bloody foot and went straight to Chief's house after the sheriff came to his and met him at the cement pond in the front yard, where Chief was feeding cracker crumbs to a huge old marbled white goldfish. (Even though the odds calculated by half a dozen shrimpers standing around a driverless truck said he should be dead, Chief was the only one who escaped without a lick of blood spilled. Lucky lucky man. Too bad his son Archie Don didn't have half his luck.)

"Well, I hope you're satisfied," Daddy said. "Now you got not only attempted *capital* murder charges and theft of a boat, you got one ol' crazed woman knocked in the head. And nearly drowned your own granddaughter too. And look at her foot there. Oyster shells nearly took the whole bottom off. Hope it was worth your while. Oh yeah, breaking and entering. I forgot that one."

"Oooh, that's a bunch of bull crap and you know it," Chief said. "All we done was try to get away with our lives while they were still our own. Is that alarming them in Austin now? Getting their gills in a big fat uproar?"

"Outrunning a game warden's boat when he wants you to stop is—"

"That is the man that killed your brother! And besides . . . you've done the same! What was it you done that time? Oooh, you know, that time that man drowned?"

Daddy said, "That man was already dead. No drowning to it. Monoxide poisoning."

"That ain't what I'm talking about, Billy. What you so touchy about anyhow? I'm talking about being on the other side of the reef when the game warden said different. Breaking THE GAME WARDEN LAW! Oh my, ain't we awful!"

"I didn't—"

"Oh yeah, you did . . . other side of the reef. Besides, we didn't even know he wanted us to stop, did we, girlie? Couldn't hear nothin' above the roar of that got dang engine. Loud got dang thing. No wonder he couldn't sell that boat."

"He was chasing y'all across the bay! Now, ain't that a clear enough sign? A boat running along behind y'all? Why you think he done that?"

"Why you think he killed Archie Don? Huh? And how 'bout Sambo? Why you think he done that?"

Daddy stood with his hands on his hips and his mouth opened and closed like a curtain falling on a stage. Finally he said he'd talked with the sheriff. Off the record, of course. And the sheriff told him it was none of the sheriff department's business messing in game-warden business, which was the exact same thing as messing with Austin's business. Those two were best left entirely alone. But the sheriff was telling Daddy—off the record, of course—that the sheriff department couldn't prove nothing. Nothing at all. Lots and lots of this and that; bits about the wife running around, all manner of stuff about men being seen with her, at a honky-tonk, riding in a car and nearly on top of a man down around the cemetery road. Then a little something in a road somewhere. But proof that the game warden shot Archie Don? And Sambo? And he wasn't even gonna talk about Chief and his dreams. That little vapor thing. Nope. Nope. He needed *physical* evidence and he couldn't prove the game warden had a rifle let alone shot a man. And that wife causing all the problems? Whyyy she was meek as a little lamb when it came to accusing her husband of anything. Probably find them both sitting side by side, holding hands, in the Baptist church next Sunday morning. He wouldn't be a bit surprised. Besides, and this was the kicker for a law officer trying to show motive: Why just Sambo? How come the game warden didn't shoot a half-dozen others if wifely infidelity was the reason he shot Sambo? 'Cause there was a half-dozen others he could've shot. Maybe more.

"*Because,*" Chief said, spitting the words, "that game warden'd be a serial killer if he done 'em all in. There'd be a massacre and we'd be burying half the town. Shoot a mile, Billy! He'd be stirrin' up stink clear to Austin, bringing down the Texas Rangers, trucking down their horses so they could hitch a ride on our boats. That's why he picked Sambo. Because he was the dumbest one of the lot that even his own wife don't miss. Let him be the dead man if there's gotta be a dead man."

"And Archie was in the wrong place at the wrong time?"

"Yep, that's the general idea."

Daddy said he was finished. He'd heard enough. Don't know why he even mentioned the sheriff. He could see it wasn't changing Chief. And he quit thinking what Chief would do next. Guess he'd just let it happen. It was either that or let the sheriff stick Chief in jail and tie him in a chair in a straightjacket. And if he did that, would he stay? Probably not. Probably talk a guard into cutting him loose and stealing him a boat. But Chief sure wasn't getting any more help from girls crawling through the window.

So I was moved right in with Grandma, where I was told to lounge on a homemade quilt with my foot propped up for exactly two days. Which I did and watched Aunt Silver, through the window, pulling heads off chickens for supper. Aunt Silver was in the chicken-wringing business now, replacing Grandma as the chief executioner ever since she and her husband and two kids had moved in with their little silver trailer that they parked underneath an ash tree in Grandma's yard with the door slung open at all times because a little silver anything in Texas was a heat gizmo—especially the grated metal steps leading up to the trailer. Stepping onto those prickly high points of metal with bare feet when the sunlight was bearing hard through the ash branches would brand you like an iron.

In God's Texan Army, Aunt Silver was a machine gunner, assaulting the stronghold of the devil by singing gospel songs to the inmates in jail, gathering food and clothing for the Church of Jesus Loves You's fellowship hall, attending a prayer circle for the sick folks in bed and in the hospital, organizing a vacation Bible school for half the town's kids and upsetting the Baptists and the Methodists in the process, teaching a Sunday-school class, and riding with Sister Pearl to the Women's Missionary Council. But an hour before meals, she'd dart into her trailer kitchen and fry up a big plate of chicken or a pot of chicken and dumplings plus fried okra coated in cornmeal, mashed squash covered in butter, mashed potatoes covered in white gravy, and fresh biscuits covered with homemade grape jelly.

Grandma wouldn't eat none of it, saying it was a sin to waste so much food and who was gonna eat all that food? It was enough to feed a starving nation! And why did she have to do all that merrymaking? (Aunt Silver cooked with a glad glad heart.) Grandma believed that the Bible in general, and Jesus in particular, condemned eating, drinking, and being merry. Then she quoted Proverbs 23:20–21, which said if you were a glutton you might as well put a knife to your throat, and Aunt Silver quoted a Bible verse back at her, saying he who brings a hearty appetite has eternal life and will be fit and ready for the Final Day. John, Chapter 6.

In Idaho, Aunt Silver's position had been a lot clearer and certainly more appreciated than in Texas. On off-church days in Idaho she was the dispenser of food, clothing, and salvation for the entire homeless sector stretching from Idaho to the Oregon border. In a long unheated building located beside their church parking lot and a room, too, inside their own parsonage that was so cram-packed with boxes that a homeless person could only crack the door open a little and shove himself in, strangers could find racks and racks of clothes and boxes and bins of dusty misshapen shoes.

Aunt Silver was a Jesus lover, a tongue-speaking, hand-on-the-top-of-your-head Holy Roller who believed the Tribulation with its gutters of blood was coming very very soon. And when the Lord Jesus came on that Glad Day, he'd lift her outta her five-inch high-heel shoes at the very same instance Satan and his minions were buzzing to earth like giant winged mosquitoes to hatch the Tribulation, and hallelujah, she could eat fried seafood all she wanted. And she wouldn't have to peel those shrimp or shuck those oysters. No, sir, and no, ma'am. She'd rule and she'd judge in heaven, but she would not work no more. But until that glory-time day (or night), she'd just have to tarry and pray pray pray.

So Aunt Silver checked her church calendar and found she had another day to give to the Lord and it took her less than a week to find out about Brother Dynamite's church on the river and another day to find out where it was located and what time it started. The snake part didn't bother her at all. What was good enough for the Bible was good enough for her.

Good enough for me too, she decided after she'd had a long talk with Momma over the kitchen table about my troubling misadventures through the bedroom window and lying in the road and hanging from the trees by my toes and yanking off towel racks when something wasn't going just right. Sounded like willfulness to her. She didn't dare think about devil-inspired willfulness. Do not go there. Besides, she had two kids and her experience was that the will of a child was different from the will of God and of the parent, too, and on matters of lifelong importance (and some not so important) right choices had to be made. You don't abdicate that role to a willful child. Besides, she held Sister Pearl's conviction that I was meant for the Christian life, most probably the wife of a Pentecostal preacher or missionary in the Congo. After all, I was named Silver— her namesake—and the Lord had sent an oyster shell to cut my foot so I could live with Grandma for a while. That said it right there. A sign straight from God. And Aunt Silver knew a lot about signs. It was the same as God talking to you, she said. And that's the way he talked to her when she needed prayer on Luann, the more willful of her two kids. Signs showing what she did and how she got there. God knew it all.

Luann was part of Aunt Silver's twin set that she dressed in matching colors. They were the same height, had the same color of light brown hair, and had the same thin face with a lick and a promise of freckles, but their personalities were different as night and day. Luann was thin and wore cat's-eye glasses, and the tilt of one lip was pretty but was sometimes mistaken by her mother for mischief. I think it was fair to say that adventure was hitching a ride on that lip. Anyhow, Luann talked as fast as any cow auctioneer sitting astraddle a fence that we'd ever heard and she called everybody (man, woman, and child) You guys, you guys. Naturally, she hitched up with Sheena, Queen of the Jungle, because Luann liked boys and cars and, especially, boys *in* cars and knew everyone available before, during, and after church before the dust even settled on their little silver trailer.

Luann allowed me to hang around her because of my inability to refuse anybody anything and because I believed every cotton-picking thing I heard. (Polite people would say I was gullible.) Anyhow, my talents knew no bounds and surprised even Luann. I believed every story she told me: fanciful encounters with total strangers and why she just said what she just said to her mother and why I should do the same. Once she sat me down at their trailer's kitchen table with two coffee cups in front of me (Aunt Silver didn't believe in coffee drinking but she made instant coffee for her coffee-drinking sisters; she said instant coffee was half the sin of perked coffee because it took half the time to make), and she said, Guess which cup has sugar and what cup has salt and if you guess wrong, you eat the salt.

So I ate a coffee cup of salt.

Leroy was a horse of a different color. He didn't have a war raging. He sat entirely within the glad glances of his momma and daddy—a handsome boy that rode bikes, shot BB guns, and climbed trees to cut the heads off baby birds while we stood underneath, hollering, Don't do it, don't do it. He did it anyhow, grinning good-naturedly as he showed us his pocketknife, the sharp edge open and bloody. Then he wiped the blade on his blue jeans and tucked it inside his pocket.

AUNT Silver decided on Wednesday night for a visit to the river church, and for a Pentecostal youth minister and a preacher's wife, Aunt Silver dressed pretty fancy, especially to be tromping around the swamp at night. She wore high heels with pointy toes, but even with five-inch heels ending in dagger points that nearly tripped her every time she stepped onto her grated trailer steps, she was only five feet tall. Uncle Orville was taller but he wasn't coming, he said. He was an Idaho man and Idaho men don't cotton to snakes. He'd just stay there in the trailer with the kids. He'd read his Bible.

Aunt Silver said, "Sweetheart! Get out here in this car!"

Uncle Orville hollered, "I'm reading my Bible!"

"Sweeetheaaart, get out heeere!"

Uncle Orville worked himself into the couch's cushions and turned his shoulder just enough in a vague little nothing movement that looked like he was turning his back on her. Oh, that did it!

Aunt Silver yelled, Sweetheart, get out here and give me a kiss good-bye or you are gonna regret it, and he said, Ummm, and Aunt Silver said, Sweetheart! Come here and give me a kiss. Finally Uncle Orville got up off the couch, grumbling, Oooh, all right! And he came out and gave her a smack on the lips and Aunt Silver smiled.

Aunt Silver drove a heavy car that could hit seventy miles an hour in a few seconds or more but she said she had never burned up a motor. They just wore out on her. And only once did she have an accident and that was when Uncle Orville was climbing in the passenger's side of the car and Aunt Silver's high-heel shoe got caught on the gas pedal and she drug him clear across the yard while he was still hanging on the car door. He apologized later about climbing in that car so slow.

She started the car and it labored at first and then purred like a kitten. "Get in," she said, "this ol' veeehicle won't kick you to pieces. It's built heavy as a train."

It was doubly dark inside and with little metal hoods over the window to keep light that was out there *out*. We were virtual prisoners of the night. Nothing like I'd ever seen but Aunt Silver said that was because it was an Idaho car. They had to have something pretty heavy to pull their silver travel trailer across America and through all those mountain passes. I was riding shotgun in the front seat and not only because Uncle Orville said somebody had to watch Aunt Silver's lead foot (short as she was and barely making the pedal, she had enough of a high heel to speed) but also because somebody had to watch for the right dirt road, the second road past Hogs Bayou, and the wild hogs (there had been a dozen wild hogs killed and vehicles smashed by head-on collisions with each other) and to make sure we didn't run off into the river when we headed back because Aunt Silver had a condition where she went to sleep at the wheel.

So we went down the second dirt road that was a truck's width and never you mind the ruts, because that was to be expected in river-bottom country. Lucky lucky us, it wasn't raining. Anyhow, we were definitely outta town and past the county line and we better be careful when climbing out of the car tonight because no telling what kinda snake was crawling around and wanting to take a shot at our ankles. It was a dizzy, winding ride with river fog and willow trees and suddenlike Holy Ghost apparitions flitting through our headlights at every corner we turned. Then the river church came up sudden and out of nowhere and Aunt Silver skidded into some elephant ears where half a dozen trucks with fenders in various stages of rust and back ends piled high with torn-up nets, busted shrimp doors, and chains were parked.

Even before we got out the door I could see there was a race going on between the mosquitoes and the river floating by and the river shack, and it was a race for who was gonna last the longest, but the shack didn't know it. The shack just thought it was a church with ten men and three women sitting in chairs and fixing to sing some songs. Wasn't nobody but Aunt Silver in her high-heel shoes paying the river and the mosquitoes a lick of attention and she kicked every time a honeysuckle vine or an elephant ear grabbed her foot and she slapped a dozen mosquitoes before she got in the front door.

FOURTEEN

Brother Dynamite didn't look at us, but if he had, he'd probably done the same thing he was doing now: his face locked into whatever was coming from the ceiling and melting him down and paying nobody, whatso-ever, a bit of attention. A guitar picker was standing nearby but he wasn't playing. Maybe he was waiting on another picker, but mostly folks seemed to be waiting on Brother Dynamite. Watching his direction. What was Brother D gonna do next. Lots of guesswork when you're dealing with the Holy Ghost. Just in case though, they'd brought in a half-dozen snakes of their own in wooden boxes with wire meshes and shoeboxes and glass jars and every one was shoved under the benches they were sitting on.

Aunt Silver marched right down to the front bench in her high-heel shoes and didn't show a bit of shyness about scooting folks over, getting a lady to move her purse, getting a man to get up and give her his seat and then go back and stand at a window. Then if that wasn't bad enough she turned and motioned for me to come down and sit beside her. But I stood in the doorway, half in, half out. The night at my back, the mosquitoes doing the Evil One's bidding. I wasn't going no place. I didn't move. Sometimes that's the best policy. Just don't move.

The mosquitoes inside weren't nearly as bad as they were outside, but they were bad. Most everybody was slapping at a mosquito or scratching a mosquito's bite. One woman had a ragged songbook she was using to fan the mosquitoes away, but the look on her face said she knew it was totally useless. Only Brother Dyanmite, dressed in a long-sleeved white shirt with dark blue pants and brown shoes and a swarm of mosquitoes hovering over him like an insect halo from heaven, hadn't moved a muscle. Praise Jesus. He was living right.

Finally he looked down at us—mild sweat stains on his shirt and a gentle dream somewhere in his eyes. "Rise up from your places," he said, "wherever y'all are . . . sisters there on the chair and brother sitting in the window and y'all on the bench too. Rise up with me and get a vision of Jesus. Then y'all reign on high and judge the world and the angels too. It ain't just snake handling we're doing here in this little river church. When the Holy Spirit gets to falling out of the ceiling like manna from heaven, falling so fast and hard that you can hardly swallow, you can hardly hear your heartbeat it gets so loud in your ears, beating you down . . . oooh, Lord, beat me down. Beat me up, Lord, beat me anywhere you like. . . . Oh hallelujah. Well, anyhow, brothers and sisters, when that happens, when that commences to happen, I can't predict what I'm liable to do. I'm just waiting on directions, waiting upon the power of the Holy Ghost, and if he wants me to take up them snakes then I'm gonna take up them snakes whether I want to or not. Them ones y'all brought and some I got here myself. A whole carload of constables couldn't keep me from handling them snakes if the HOLY GHOST wants it! HALL-E-LUJAH! I do it all in Jesus's precious name anyhow. And I ask it too, precious Jesus, in your name. Amen.

"Now. All y'all new here, and I see a couple, there on the front row, sister . . . bless your heart and thank ya for coming. I'm gonna say a little something for educational purposes about these snakes. There under the pew and this here cage behind me. I built it myself. I got a few more in the back room there. It's all the same, though. Snakes is snakes if yore afraid. A few won't hurt you too bad, but some will kill you outright if your faith ain't strong and your eye ain't on the Lord. So when y'all go talking to y'all's brothers and sisters in the Lord tomorrow or whenever y'all do it, I want the truth of this church and what we do here to come out right. Not some big ol' fanciful yarn y'all made up on purpose just to amuse yoreself.

"Now. First thing, some of y'all are probably doubting Thomases—oooh, that's okay, don't matter no mind to me—saying stuff like, 'Oooh, those snakes don't bite him 'cause of his warm hands.' Well, saints, warm hands will *agitate* a snake. Why you think they crawl in the summertime and go into hiding in the wintertime? 'Cause they like it? NO, 'cause heat aggravates them! Or that snake don't bite him because of the guitar music or the songs folks are singing. Snakes are deaf, folks. Music don't affect them. Then some of y'all thinking, Oh, he ain't afraid because he's done it before. Gotten himself snakebit and develped an *immunity* to snakes. You like that word? *Immunity?* Means I *can't* get sick no matter how many snakes bite me. The more the better. Well, that ain't true neither. That's a lie. I ain't been bit yet, but I can tell you for sure that if I *do*, I'll be setting myself up in the *next* bite to get the worse bodily reaction ever.

"Saints, we ain't just playing here. It's FIRE we're dealing with. DYNAMITE and FIRE! Ain't nothing tame
about this church because there's nothing TAME about
the Bible. Just sayin' it like it is, folks. Sayin' it like it is.

"Now. Folks. I ain't a bit worried. The Lord says he is my
shepherd, my rod and my staff. He will protect me. He will
let me lie down beside still waters. He says those snakes
shall DO ME NO HARM. Is that clear enough? Jesus gave
me the Gift of Dynamite and I'm taking up snakes as his
commandment. He's got other ones too. Thou shalt not
commit adultery, thou shalt not have any graven images.
A few more others too, but the commandment he gave me
was Mark 16, verse 18. Thou shalt take up serpents.

"Now, some wordly men—and women too—might
consider that commandment a fairy tale and say I'm lying
to y'all or the Bible is lying . . . or *somebody is lying*. But
Holy Spirit–filled believers know the truth: the Holy Spirit
dictated the whole Bible without taint or error. The Bible
dropped from heaven as a sacred meteor, tumbling from
the hands of God, and that, my friends in Jesus, means the
Bible should be read as literally as possible.

"Now, I ain't gonna stand here and lie to y'all and say I
never handled snakes before. 'Cause I have. And I haven't.
That ain't lying, is it? Talking outta both sides of your
mouth? Truth is complicated sometimes. So I'm gonna tell
y'all the gospel truth but it's a little complicated, just like
I said. Now. When I was little, my daddy—in Florida—he
handled snakes at a little Pentecostal church and sometimes he'd travel and handle them someplace else. There
was a whole bunch of them snake handlers in Florida at

the time—oh, I don't know, maybe there was twenty or so of them—and they'd get together and tell each other places where they were gonna be next. Preaching and a little handling if the spirit was moving them. Speaking in tongues. Dancing in the spirit.

"This all got started because Daddy had got the spirit and was saved early on, and when he seen a man in Tallahassee handle snakes, he started doing it too. Keeping live snakes in the house. Making cages for them, feeding them lizards and little birds, little rats. It got so bad that he couldn't see a snake anywhere and not stop. Even if it crossed the road in front of his truck. He'd get out, walk up to it, and squat down, and in a low voice that only the snake could hear, he'd say something like, 'Which way you want it? Which way?' Then if the snake didn't say—and there's plenty of snakes that don't—he'd make a little deal with them. 'You go right, then no harm done. I'll take you to church with me tonight and let you loose tomorrow. But if it's to the left, then it's something else. I gotta go back in the truck and get me a stick and kill you. You make up your mind now, which way you wanna go.' Daddy would kneel for a long time that way, just like he was praying, his face inches from the snake, both hands in the sand. Then he'd get up and walk back to us and say, 'Me and Jesus talked with it,' and he'd smile.

"Then one summer this big ol' bugger of a rattlesnake got loose from its cage—it was big and *mean* and rest-less—and it bit Momma on the thumb and she died real quick. Thirty minutes and she was gone. It was my brother that walked to the nearest house and telephoned the sheriff that our momma was dead and would the sheriff come, and when they reached the house, it was my brother who met them at the door and asked them to come in. . . . Like it was nothing. Like they were coming for supper or something. I don't know, maybe he was affected by it all. Got touched in the head by it. Probably was.

"Anyhow, that snake was still somewhere loose in the house and Daddy was off somewhere, maybe he was down the river, but he come back later after the state had already sent a woman to remove me and my brother, saying the snakes were endangering our lives. Or something like that. And I guess they were. One sure killed my momma—and brothers and sisters, just so y'all know—that's *one* reason why I ain't ever gonna allow any momma with a bunch of kids, or *one* kid, to get up here and handle snakes. Not tonight, not tomorrow night, not *ever*. I don't care how spirit-filled she says she is. I don't *ever* wanna look in the eyes of some kid whose momma just died from a snakebite. I don't wish that hard-luck story on nobody.

"Anyhow, back to the subject. 'Bout six months after the state of Florida took us away, they sent us back again. But I sure hated them snakes. I sure did. I'd kill ever' one if I could've caught 'em, but I was still just a baby. I was seven, barely out of diapers, and a momma dead. Think I didn't hate them snakes? And the daddy that brung 'em? I hated them all! I was gonna fight them and Daddy too.

"I had a little oleander switch I carried with me and I'd beat it back and forth against the bushes, against the porch, against the climbing wisteria vine alongside the back door that was the only thing Momma got growing before she died. And I'd yell—shoot, I'd yell it everywhere—'I'm just gonna have to whip you. Yore just gonna get it.'

"Daddy got kinda crazy after the snakebite. He put up a sign in his truck saying Christmas was for devils and later on he locked us in the closet for reasons nobody could figger. Maybe spare the rod and spoil the child. That type of thing. I thought maybe he just didn't want us in school learning something different from what he was preaching 'cause it was the missing-school part that finally got him in trouble. Well, that plus the closet. Still, nobody really knew why he done it. Not even the jail people that came and got him and sent him to jail for a couple months, but then he came back and we didn't see any change in him. We still had the snakes. They were in boxes all over the house. Some in the closet, a couple in the bathroom. Me and my brother shared a bed and there were three or four boxes shoved under there. Daddy was always getting more snakes. In our spare time too, that's what me and my brother were doing. Always hunting scraps of wood and screen and tearing latches off screen doors so Daddy could build his cages. He'd load us both in his pickup and he'd drop me off around some local dump spot, but my brother . . . Daddy let him out at other people's houses and told him to go on up to their screen doors and ask them for broken windows parts, old screen doors, pieces from their old chicken pens. He didn't care. My brother quit school entirely after that and started decking on Daddy's shrimp boat. I guess he figured he was better off on a boat than getting locked up in that closet again. He was pretty good at it, too, so Daddy started trusting him more and more with that boat, finally letting him go out on his own and holding a wheel like he was a man of forty when actually he was only fourteen. Daddy had his snake-handling meetings he was going to anyhow, and that was taking up a lot of his time. Sometimes he was gone for a week. Which was fine with us. Me and my brother were doing just fine by ourselves. I'd run a string of lines in the river that I'd check ever' morning and after I came back from school in the evening, so I was catching catfish and my brother would bring in a little shrimp or some crabs off the boat. With shrimp and crab, all you need is a pot of boiling water and you got yourself a meal, anyhow. So we weren't starving. But then Daddy would come home from a trip and then the trouble would start again. Usually it was because of some leftover preachin' that rode back in the truck with him from a church meeting and he brung it in the house with him. If it was night, he'd drag us both out of bed and tell us to kneel down around the kitchen table. There was a kerosene lamp on the table and he'd stick one of those big yellow rattlesnakes that was another something he brung from the truck along with that preaching and he laid it across the table alongside the light and a Bible alongside that, then he'd pray that Jesus would heal our lame heads. He said every child born in the world was lame in three places: in his head, in his will, and in his affections. And if he could heal the lame head, then the Holy Spirit would heal the will and the affections. Something like that. Anyhow, that was the closest I ever got to understanding why he didn't want us in school.

"Pretty pitiful, ain't it, brothers and sisters? Y'all think Jesus was gonna fix that broken relationship I just told y'all about? For me? Do it all for me with nothing on my part but just lazing around, hating everything being done to me? Well, y'all know what the Bible says. . . . The blood of Jesus don't blot out any sin between man and man that they can't make right themselves. But if they can't make the wrongs right, then the blood graciously covers. So Jesus is a gentlemen, brothers and sisters. Don't know whether y'all knew that or not, but Jesus is a gentleman! He graciously covers when you can't do it for yourself.

"Now. Whadda 'bout my ol' daddy, you say? Well, it's too late for my daddy. He's already gone and what's done is done. I can't make that wrong right again and Jesus knows it and knows how it was tormenting me. So his blood come and covered it. He made *riiight* on the *wrooong* and I'm a different man for it. What I was in that jail cell . . . wanting to kill kill kill, stab a man's life out with a screwdriver! Well, Jesus took all that hate and despair. . . . Yesss, he took it away. . . . So if Jesus told me right now to drink the battery acid out of those batteries in the trucks out there, whyyy, I'd do it! I'd do it! Oh hallelujah, I'd do it and praise Jesus doing it."

It was pretty clear to me that the river church was getting crosswise with Aunt Silver. Here the river church (with Brother Dynamite officiating) had crossed off women on snake handling. And if he crossed off snake handling, what would would he cross off next? So I was sure Aunt Silver wouldn't be back here again. No nighttime road trip. No cranny hole for Aunt Silver to tell her Bible stories. She was part of the snake onlookers just like the rest of us.

Brother Dynamite had quit talking and he motioned for the guitar pickers (the single guitar player had found another picker and two of them stood in a tight corner with barely room for them to stretch their guitars out right) to play a song. They picked "Lily of the Valley," and while they sang the verse, the rest of the church joined in on the chorus.

> *I have found a friend in Je-sus, he's ev-'ry-thing to me,*
> *He's the fair-est of ten thou-sand to my soooul,*
> *The Lil-y of the Val-ley, in him a-lone I see,*
> *All I need to cleanse and make me fuuully whole.*
> *In sor-row he's my com-fort, in troub-le he's my stay,*
> *He tells me ev-'ry care on him to roooll,*
>
> Chorus:
> *He's the Lil-y of the Val-ley of the Val-ley, the bright*
> * and morn-ing star,*
> *He's the faaair-est of ten thou-sand to my soooul.*

The pickers went from that song to another, switching chords as easily as a man flipping a coin through his fingers, winding first around the thumb, then the pointing finger, then the coin showing up between the last two fingers.

> *Living by faith in Jesus above,*
> *Trusting, confiding in his great love,*
> *Safe from all harm in his sheltering arms,*
> *I'm living by faith and feel no alarm.*

Everybody crowded to the front and a few forayed into
jumping up and down in place. That left only me at the
back with a wallowed-out screen where the man that Aunt
Silver had got to move had sat and now it was empty so
I went and plopped myself down in the window and idly
slapped mosquitoes. It wasn't late. Probably only two
hours since Aunt Silver had plowed into the elephant ears,
so that meant it was *early* in the service. Grandma (unlike
Momma) believed the length of a sermon indicated how
good the Holy Ghost's juices were flowing and its strength.
(And it also indicated the *high* voltage on her radio so
after a fiery two-hour religious broadcast, she sometimes
unplugged the radio to let it cool down. She didn't want
her house to burn down.) I'd been in lots of Christmas and
New Year's Eve services where it went all night and ran
into the next day. Preaching, praying, singing, testifying,
speaking in tongues, healings of all sorts with cloths soaked
in olive oil and placed on your head, midnight suppers in
the fellowship hall, two A.M. victory marches around the
church, foot washing (men only) at the altar, reenactments
of Baby Jesus's birth with teenage boys in borrowed house-
coats and cute little kids in cardboard angel wings singing
"Silent night, holy night" to a young girl holding a baby
doll in front of a makeshift curtain made of two bedsheets,
and, once (this under the direction of a visiting evangelist wearing a light blue, three-piece, polyester pantsuit),
an elaborate reenactment of hell. The overhead church
lights were covered with red cloths and four members of
the church played a backslidden daddy with two kids and a
good saintly wife and the family was walking nice and easy

down Life's Road (the middle church aisle) when suddenly the daddy's grabbed by two devils (two church members dressed in red) who drag him screaming off to hell. There was much wailing and screaming in the congregation.

So my experience with preaching and preachers was that the service lasted as long as it lasted and the longer the better. Holy Ghost working was just Holy Ghost working and only the devil inspired would dare to call themselves tired.

I wasn't tired. I was just sitting down, the better to see and slap mosquitoes and watch Brother D get into the snake-handling part. He reached under the shrimp-door pulpit for a large square box that was screened on the top and had some brass tacks pounded in on the side, spelling out JESUS SAVES. Then—no surprise no surprise—as he lifted the screen top, Aunt Silver stumbled up from her front-row bench and threw her head and arms so violently back that the pins came undone from her hair and showered down her back like hard rain. She wept a waterfall and prayed with her strong short arms wobbling in the air.

"Oooh, Lord in all your mercy, come down tooonight and protect this servant of yours from the venomous fangs of Satan's worst viper. Oooh, Lord, just like you did in the olden biblical days when you sent the angel down to wrap his heavenly wings around Shadrach, Meshach, and Abednego in King Nebuchadnezzar's fiery furnance . . . and like that time, oooh, Lord, when you sealed the hungry mouths of lions when Daniel was thrown in the lions' den with a stone rolled across the opening and all because he prayed before you, oooh, Lord, and not King Darius. Lord, we're asking you to come down and do the same thing here toooonight.

Oooh, Jesus, wrap your earthly servant *this very second* in a white cloak of blessed love and protection and seal the mouth of these venomous vipers! Oooh, shandameia shandalamikey . . . oh shandala shandala."

Brother Dynamite didn't lose his focus for a second. He shouted, "Praise Jesus for his blood that cleans up, the Holy Ghost that fills up, and the dynamite that blows up." In the name of JEEESUS he was picking up these snakes and it didn't matter if he was getting them in the middle or catching them by their heads or their tails. "It don't matter," he said, and he lifted two big rattlesnakes high above his head and immediately two snake tails dropped on either side of Brother Dynamite's thrust-out arms and whipped around his chest for a second, then they curled up his back. The interesting part, though, was high in his hands and nearly in the rafters. (The church wasn't all that tall, with barely room for a standing average-sized man, although at the peak an average-sized man could have stood with a cowboy hat on if he happened to have one. But he wouldn't have. These were fishermen and fishermen rarely wore hats even though they got sores from working in the sun all day long.) Two bulky black heads moved left to right, left to right. No big hurry. Left to right, left to right, whooosh whooosh, flicking their tongues. Then Brother D brought his arms down and put the snake heads level with his eyes. The rattlers really started buzzing but Brother D paid the rattling no mind. He was like a kid on the front porch playing with a Slinky tied to a dynamite stick, and the Slinky/dynamite stick flipped down one step, then the next, and never quite left one step before it hit another.

I had seen enough of those snake devils.

LordJesusLordJesusLordJesus. I backed out the door. LordJesusLordJesusLordJesus. I stood awhile in the dark. LordjesusLordJesusLordJesus. Not watching the church. LordJesusLordJesusLordJesus. Not watching the river. LordJesusLordJesusLordJesus. I walked over to Aunt Silver's car and got in.

Soon as I sat down, I saw the game warden leaning across a truck and picking through a net. He shoved the net aside and grabbed something else. He was three trucks over, bordered on two sides by chest-high elephant ears, and the only thing between him and me were a dozen (barely visible and unintentional) neatly made truck ruts.

I squirmed down in the car seat with my head barely above the dashboard and deliberated on a run to the elephant ears. Then a mad run to the back door. And then what? Run in and tell the fishermen that a killer game warden was picking through their nets and maybe they oughta rush out and find that game warden with his thumb still in their nets?

Better to sit still and hide inside the Idaho car with its shaded windows. My foot was hurting anyhow. So I hid, but I knew in a second that was wrong because I warted myself silly, thinking he was seeing me one minute, then not seeing me the next. Up and down, up and down. Did he see me? Nope. Yes he did, yes he did. My foot was hurting plenty good now and my breath climbed higher and higher in my chest until it sounded like thunder to my ears.

Finally the game warden moved from the trucks and

went around the back side of the river church, where I thought—wrong again!—that the shack was so backed up to the river that only a water moccasin or a man in a skiff could enter that way. He knew better.

Eventually the church let out and a few early stragglers came outside and stood around a bit, but the mosquitoes were thick and biting hard so they ran for their trucks and rolled up the windows. Aunt Silver bustled out, talking loud with a woman and still talking as she followed her to a truck where the woman got in, sat a second with the truck door open, then pulled the door shut, rolled the window up, and said bye-bye to Aunt Silver and "Let's go" to her husband all in the same breath. That just gave Aunt Silver the excuse to go back inside the church.

If I didn't count Brother D's borrowed car, we were the only vehicle left. I didn't know where the game warden's truck was parked. Maybe he came by skiff and parked at the back door. Maybe he was visiting with Aunt Silver. That would be a conversation I'd hate to miss. I looked outside and the leaves overhead were still and unmoving as rocks in the river. The wind was zero too, but that was nothing; the wind could be blowing a gale on the bay with whitecaps everywhere, but inside River Bottom Country the ropy vines and oak and willow and hackberry trees cut off the wind same as the sunlight. No wonder the river church looked like a burned-out hull. Dark and skeletal. Then Aunt Silver swung open the car door, plunked herself and her purse behind the wheel, rummaged around in the bag for a second, pulled out a flowered handkerchief, wet the ends with some spit, and wiped her face. Suddenly she turned and said, "You little brat! Why didn't you tell me Brother Dynamite's brother is a game warden?"

I said, Why, why I didn't know it, and she said, Brat! You did too. And lying will send you to hell same as for stealing.

FIFTEEN

This was my first inkling that Anthony Perkins was the end-all to beat end-alls.

I was sitting in the weeds where it's always summer—even in the dead of winter. So there was plenty sun. Not much cold. That's what I liked. Anyhow, Anthony came and sat on his heels. He was wearing rattlesnake boots and black pants and a white shirt. Once upon a time, Anthony Perkins was on a picture-show screen but now he was sitting in the weeds. He'd been a long time coming down my road, he said. He'd been coming since I was nine. You're ten now, he said.

He was right. I was ten and a nearly grown girl and recently sleeping by myself. My oldest brother had joined the Navy and Momma had given me his tiny room with the metal bed that I had already chiseled a message on (YOU WILL DISAPPEAR IN THREE DAYS) with a bent fork prong.

Anthony scooted closer and got right to the point. He said he wanted to know what I was doing and I said I was waiting on hell to send a message up through the dirt. It wasn't entirely a lie. I was waiting on a clear message from Archie Don to send to Chief, and since by everybody's account Archie Don was sitting on a boat in a lake of hellfire it just made sense. Anthony seemed unconcerned. Then he sort of hummed, then he got lost in his humming, then he said he was saving one doomed girl from damnation and it was me and he sure hoped I knew it.

Well, as long I didn't have to go nowhere, I said. I didn't want to go nowhere, be anywhere, let my light shine, save my soul, save my daddy's soul, save Archie Don's soul. I mean, I didn't want to be. If I had to be, then I wanted to be like that time when I liked cement.

Move over, Anthony said. (He was like that. Real sparse with his words, like he was a drought and words were the water.) So I did. But there you close the door and there it swings open on its own. That's the trouble with messages. This is what happened: my head's insides moved an inch. My handwritten message in the dirt switched from right leaning to left leaning. And in the weeds and later under the chinaberry trees (the shedding, weeping chinaberry trees) I ceased to exist. No curtains moved in my house.

We have a deal, he said, and I said we have a deal until I'm eighty years old and looking like a bunch of squashed grapes.

Okay, he said. Now a couple rules. Don't talk so much, and I said, I dooon't talk, and he said, Well, don't talk some more. And don't wear a coat, and I said, I dooon't wear a coat. Well, don't even think about wearing a coat. We don't feel nothing. Not the cold. Not hunger. So don't eat that oatmeal in the morning. It's hard anyhow. Too much cooking. Not enough water. And don't hang around your sisters. Not their girlfriends. Not their boyfriends. Not your cousins. And DON'T tell Aunt Silver nothing. She gets a reward for catching people like us. Now, pull up those weed covers and go to sleep, he said, and I said, What are you doing, are you leaving? and he said, Nawp, not me. Pretty soon even a gun couldn't drive me away. 'Cause these are perilous times, Silver. These are judgment days. So where do you stand, Silver? Which side of the line are you on? Are you with me or Jesus?

Naturally I told Aunt Silver and she said exactly the same thing about the line plus a bit about living in the final cloudburst of the Holy Spirit where demons would fall copiously from the third realm and that includes movie stars.

Anthony Perkins ain't the devil, I said. Anthony was in the picture show when I was in the second grade and he was wearing nice clothes!

Devils can get on picture shows too, she said. They can get into cars. They can dress up in regular clothes just like you and me. Anthony Perkins maybe looks like a movie star to you BUT to me—and I'm the expert and I know—he's the devil, and a devil sooo delighted that he's got one of Jesus's little missionettes in his ugly evil clutches! But don't you worry none. The Blessed Savior and the Holy Ghost has waaay too much invested in you to let the devil ruin your life.

So Aunt Silver told Brother Beller that I was under attack by the Evil One and my momma didn't know it and my daddy didn't know it and even I didn't know it. Nobody knew it except her. And now Brother Beller. Actually, Brother Beller said he saw it coming because he had the powerful, God-given ability of discernment (the awareness of nonphysical beings such as angels and demons) and he had a sneaking little suspicion I was more than just a little missionette sitting in church. I was possessed by a movie-star devil that no doubt was a carryover from the movie-show chairs that didn't get the proper anointing from the former pastor, and no doubt too that snake-handling episode by that False Prophet had provoked and loosened from the chairs the Anthony devil who grabbed the first ripe missionette for the picking! It boggled his mind.

The devil-deliverance ministry was serious serious business, he said, and even to be in this ministry you had to be a person of prayer and have a very strong indwelling of the Holy Ghost. Even Jesus didn't drive out demons except by the Holy Ghost. For safety, he and Aunt Silver had to work as a team on this devil. After all, Jesus had sent out his own disciples two by two to heal the sick and cast out demons. In any case, he knew never to go into a devil-deliverance situation alone again, with a person of the opposite sex, because Satan sent out people all the time to accuse ministers of sexual misconduct and other false things. It was important that Satan never gain an advantage, so they had to be ever watchful.

The next step was binding the devil. As the Holy Ghost led them, they were to bind the devil with words like these:

"In the name and authority of the Lord Jesus Christ, we renounce all the powers of Anthony Perkins, the darkness which exists in the life of Silver. We bind this evil spirit and forbid it to operate in any way, in the name of Jesus Christ."

The final item, he said, was to determine if I was a born-again Christian like I said I was. So while Brother Beller prayed and bound the demon, Aunt Silver was to spend some time questioning me. Have you truly given your life to Jesus Christ? Would you like to? Are you aware of an occult history in your family or your daddy's people? Witchcraft? Freemasonry? Any false religion such as a belief in animal spirits? Reincarnation? Superstitions? Palm reading? Dreams coming true?

Then Aunt Silver was to explain the gospel to me and lead me to Jesus, saying things like, Jesus can set you free, Jesus can save you. Without this instruction, they couldn't properly set me free from the Anthony Perkins demonic influence. But Aunt Silver was to keep it very simple because the Anthony demon would most likely try to work overtime to confuse their minds with irrelevant movie-star information.

They were lucky they knew this demon's name. Usually they didn't know. One, because it's not practical to ask a hundred demons possessing a person what all their names are, and two, because demons just can't be trusted to give out the right information. Usually they just called the demon by whatever area it influenced. So demons of fear, lust, smoking, big-headedness, movie-show watching, dancing, and so on could be commanded to leave using just those names. For example, you could say, "You, spirit of dancing, come out in Jesus's name!" or "I command you, spirit of lust, to loosen her in Jesus's name!"

In all likelihood, though, they would have a successful deliverance and I would vomit up the Anthony devil. That is, if I was *cooperatin'* I would vomit up the devil. Demons generally nested in the stomach or chest and during a heated deliverance ministry they would move up to the throat and leave through the mouth in all manner of ways: coughing, yawning, tears coming to the eyes, twitching mouth, cursing, vomiting, and spitting. At no time was I to mention the name of Jesus or pray in tongues. I should only focus my mind on Jesus and vomit out that demon. A demon can't leave a person if that person's mouth was busy praying or had the name of Jesus on her lips.

But just in case it started to go bad, Aunt Silver was to create a diversion—PRAISE GOD and SING SONGS! Demons hated that! It made them feel very bad and they wanted to get up and leave. So just before Brother Beller commanded that Anthony demon to leave, Aunt Silver was to really get into praising God and singing songs and, if at all possible, encourage me to vomit that devil out by sticking a finger down my throat.

This is what happens when deliverance fails.

I was on the flip side of Rapture. On the dark side of life. Well, at least everywhere I went, Anthony went along for the ride. Hiding in the closet. Underneath the bed and hanging from the iron bedsprings. Where once was Jesus, now was Anthony. I had a new revelation too. I would be dead before I was seventeen and, more than likely, hit by a falling plane.

Aunt Silver said Brother Beller had certainly roused that devil. Jus' look how Silver twitched in church. And that pout nearly drug the floor! Brother Beller agreed. Movie-star devils were certainly difficult to extract. If *ooonly* he could get a second chance.

But no. The Anthony devil had clearly won that round.

I went back and sat with Anthony. It was very confusing. Anthony was way bigger than me. Maybe six or seven boys bigger. Older too. Darker too. And large enough that the land, the sky, the trees, and the river looked different than they did the weeks before when I was nothing but a little missionette. I swore I didn't recognize the place but Anthony said, Oh yeah, this is it.

So the little missionette with a white shirt and a blue skirt and gold pin stuck on her shoulder sat way back in a corner (furtherest from a window) and faded out. She shrunk until she was eight inches tall and never again confused herself that she was a little girl that was gonna get bigger because that's what kids do, that's what's natural, even when a kid can't imagine it, even when a kid quit thinking it, she's gonna get bigger.

Not this kid, Anthony said. This kid had nothing to do but pull cobwebs out of the rat holes in her head until planes fell out of the sky, but sometimes when a carload of somebodies was going somewhere and one of the somebodies wanted her to come along and drink a coke, the midget missionette surfaced momentarily like an infant minnow peeking its head out on a stagnant pond.

Anthony had pleeenty to do.

In the dark, along the dust, and against the walls he took the shortest route to Chief, who was waiting, oh yes, waiting, and he got up from his worn-out sofa chair and said he wouldn't know surprise if it jumped out and bit him, but I was a good start and a sight for sore eyes.

Was my foot sore? he asked. Let him see it. Put it up

there. Then he laughed and sat down in his chair again. His hair had grown out some and the uneven ends had caught up with his shoulders and if there was a race and something in the running, well, then his hair had won. He didn't look like he had been keeping good care of himself and if he was doing any eating, sleeping, or washing he was doing it from the chair. There was a pile of dirty plates and a wadded-up towel near his foot and his cold pipe lay in a scattering of ashes, smoked out and overturned.

I said I didn't know if he'd come looking for me again because I was in a different room now. Had me a different window. And he said no, he hadn't left that chair in two weeks. Archie Don quit talking to him so all he did was go out and feed the goldfish. That was Archie Don's goldfish, he said. Thing must be twenty years old and goes through a box of crackers in a week. A regular hog, he said.

What's its name? I asked and he said, Hog Boy. Called it Hog Boy.

I said, I know something about hogs.

He said, Do you, now?

And I said, Yessir. I know a road named Hog's Road.

Oooh, Hog's *Bayou* Road. Didn't even know you knew that road. Archie Don must have told you.

So Chief decided right then and there that I must be the new spirit hunter since Archie Don didn't talk to him anymore. Maybe if I got quiet and listened good, Archie Don would jump out and talk again.

It was a good plan and a short plan. All I had to do was be quiet—which I did anyhow—and wait on Archie Don.

But naturally it was Aunt Silver who came through loudest. She was sitting with Momma and Aunt Teny and Aunt June Bug around the kitchen table and they were drinking coffee and she was drinking Royal Crown cola from a giant bottle and telling every little juicy move in the river church. All about Brother D and his older brother, who everybody now knew was the game warden, tormenting the living tar out of everybody around and how they had finally met up after all those years of being separated and at odds with one another but how they had come to an understanding of sorts because Aunt Silver had witnessed to them about the Lord's mighty plan for their lives. Just like that time when she went to Idaho to visit some kinfolks but met her future husband, Orville, instead and how they both dedicated their lives to Christ and followed his will in all things henceforth. Aunt Teny said she didn't know if it was just God's will Silver was following; seemed to be Silver's hand in most everything. And *Brother* Orville's too. And Aunt Silver said, You brat, if she had a hand in anything it was because the Holy Ghost had given her the powerful gift of discernment early on so she knew the troubled heart of Brother Dynamite when she'd last seen him at his snake-handling river ministry and it was plain as the nose on his face what she'd seen. And pray tell, Sister Silver, what was that? Aunt Teny asked, and Aunt Silver said, It was the mark of Cain! On the game warden's face? Momma screamed, and Aunt Silver said, NO, Goldie! It was Brother Dynamite's face. The mark of Cain was so visible to her discerning eye that after the service she had stayed behind to counsel him, because only by confessing our sin before Jesus are we made whole.

So you're Jesus now, are you? Aunt Teny asked, and Aunt Silver said, No, Teny, I'm not Jesus but I can fill in for Jesus when he's off on heavenly business and there's a troubled soul that's been discerned.

Troubled ain't necessarily the mark of Cain, Silver. Troubled can be worried. I'm worried too but that don't mean I'm Cain fixing to kill my brother or I'm a sinner needing to confess anything to you.

You brat, I'm talking about troubled in the soul. You know what I mean. You're just trying to be mean, you little brat. The kind of troubled I'm talking about is a sin wanting to be confessed.

Oooh, it is not. You're making this all up.

Shame on you, Teny. Mother would be ashamed if she heard you. Shame, shame on you.

Silly Silver, Silly Silver!

Momma threw her arms in the air and said if they didn't quit arguing her one good eye was gonna explode. She was gonna lose her one good eye. So Aunt Teny picked up her coffee cup and listened while Aunt Silver told Brother Dynamite's Confession.

Brother Dynamite's Confession

Ira caught the shrimp net in the wheel and actually it wasn't that big of a deal. It wasn't like that net was the only one Daddy owned because he had shrimped his whole life so he had a barn full of nets. Only problem was the rats. Rats loved nets and ate holes in the webbing big enough to drive a truck through. So if Daddy really needed another net the most he had to do was take his knife, cut out the rat holes, then fill in the holes with new webbing. So the net in the wheel was no big deal.

But word got back that the boat was broke down, net in the wheel, and tied up at some little beer joint down the river. Maybe it was a fish house too, but it sure was a beer joint. Well, that did it. Daddy grabbed me and we took off in the truck and roared off to the beer joint. It was a beer joint all right. Long skinny bar, dim light, dark bottles half-full of something sitting in every corner of the joint. And there was Ira, asleep on the floor. Somebody had thrown a quilt over him and only his rubber boots were sticking out.

Ira wasn't talking. Ira was sleeping hard so we walked out the back door and there in the yard under a giant pecan tree were three men sitting in chairs around a barbecue pit. Another man was standing at the pit with a big knife.

Man at the pit said, "That your boat down there?" And Daddy said, "Yep."

"Well, you shore got a mess. But I'll say this. That boat ain't moving. No, sir, it ain't goin' noplace."

I forgot what Daddy said but it wasn't much. Maybe two words. Daddy forgot how to talk if a rattlesnake wasn't laid down in front of him first. So we walked down to the river and I could see the boat and a shrimp net hanging straight off the stern and into the river like a giant gorilla was underwater and holding it down.

One of the men from the pecan tree came down and stood next to Daddy. He was smoking a cigarette and nodded toward the boat. "I don't believe the boat is hurt none. Just that net wound down tight. Ya know, I was here when those game wardens brought the boat in."

"Who?" Daddy said, and he looked at the man's cigarette a minute, then he frowned and looked off.

"Hell, man. The game wardens. Heard them hollering. One was on the boat with that boy and another was trailing in a skiff." Then he yanked his head toward the fish house.

"Hey, that kid your kid or he just working for you? Looks kinda young."

"What?" Daddy said.

"Ya know, that kid sleeping it off on my floor."

Daddy said nothing and the man with the cigarette in his mouth nodded. "Well, just letting you know the game warden was here. Don't know what kinda trouble he's in . . . well, besides drinking up the whole house and pissing himself."

The man looked down, then his eyes went looking at the river. After a while he said he was heading for the pecan tree to get himself a beer. So me and Daddy were stuck with the mess on the river.

Daddy hunkered down with his hands on his knees, his feet wide apart, and didn't say nothing. Then he put me on the boat to look for a washtub and when I couldn't find one he said, Go below, and

when I couldn't find one there he said, Go back to
that fish house and fetch one and don't come back
without it. So I went back, only nobody was sitting
outside in the chairs; they were all inside the beer
joint, sitting around a table, and everybody looked
at me when I drug in. Ira was still on the floor, but
his boots were toes up so I figured Ira had rolled
over at least once. I glanced over at the men and
they looked like they wanted to make barbecue
meat out of Ira so I almost didn't ask for the washtub. But I remembered Daddy so I said, Mister,
you got a washtub?

The biggest fella said he believed so and led me
outside to a broke-down refrigerated truck where
half a dozen rusty buckets held more rusty engine
parts and scraps of wire and ropes and pulleys of
every sorts, and on the floor paint cans piled to
the rafter. There were a zillion washtubs, too.
The man pried a washtub loose and slung it at my
feet and he saw a little shrimp-culling stool hanging on a bent nail and he slung that too, saying I
was gonna have one looong wait on that boat so I
might as well get comfortable.

I took the culling stool and the washtub and
walked back down to the river. Daddy was standing on the stern of the boat in his bare feet. He
had taken all the nickels and quarters and dollar
bills out of his pocket and yanked off his boots
and socks and ever'thing was in a pile on the
stern.

Daddy grabbed the washtub, edged over the stern, and slipped under the water. The washtub floated a second, then it went down and I was standing alone on the boat. I didn't see nothing in that river. Not a washtub. Not Daddy. Not nothing. So I got a flashlight out of the cabin and shoved it in the river. Then before I could yank out the flashlight Daddy was back with his tub and a knife he got from somewhere. He was breathing hard and slinging water everywhere. There was a wide purple scar where a snake had bit him once on the shoulder and I saw it a second before he took the tub and knife and went down again. I could hear the tub hitting the bottom of the boat, metal scratching metal, scratching scratching. Getting closer to that tangled net. Then the tub hit something and everything quit. It was just me and that river sounding weary as one of those church songs that never have a happening ending.

I never sat on the culling stool. I just leaned over the boat and watched the river, waiting on Daddy. The second he came up he was mad-looking and I was thinking it was me but he said it was only the tub running out of air and that tangled net. Ira too. Daddy spit some water and throwed the washtub against the boat railing but it didn't hit the railing. It just landed in the river and spun crazy. He grabbed the tub again and this time he slammed it hard against the boat and there he held it with one hand while the rest of him struggled in the current along with the sticks and the water lilies and the gators in the river.

Then he remembered me because he shouted, "Go to the gearbox and throw it in reverse." "Huh?" I said, and he said, "Reverse! Reverse! Don'tcha know how to put a boat in reverse?" His hand came up with the knife he'd been holding and he pointed to the cabin. "Git in there," he said, "and do like I say." So I got in there and looked back and Daddy nodded his head yes so I yanked a knob down and Daddy yelled, Nooo. The other one. That's the throttle!

So I yanked another knob and he said, Okay. Now c'mere and listen. So I went back and squatted next to the boat railing and he said, "When I hit the bottom of this boat with this tub—hard! Like that! Hear that! That loud noise? When I do that I want you to bump that red button in there. You see it? That red one. That's the starter button. You bump it light and that wheel down there's gonna turn in reverse. I'll kick that net out a little. I don't want much. I got some of it out already. So just a little. Don't bump it hard or it's liable to take my head off. Now git back in there." So I went back in the cabin and he and the tub and the knife slid down in the water and all that was left was the river but it wasn't a river no more. It was just a wet road with Daddy underneath and breathing in a tub.

That's when Ira come on the boat and he said, Don't worry none, Cotton. Our daddy's fixing to take a little trip up the windpipe of heaven.

It was a short summer. The shortest I ever remember. I got sent someplace. It was an accident, they said. An accident. But I still got sent someplace where lots of pieces of paper had my name. Then I got to go home to visit Ira and the second day, Ira come outside wearing Daddy's old hat that shaded his face so much I could hardly see his eyes. Under one arm he had a jar full of gasoline and in the other hand he had a matchbox and he said, Cotton, we ain't staying in this house no longer.

He was serious, he said. He had already drug out of the house everything we needed to start us a campsite somewhere else and the truck was loaded down. So what was we standing around for? Old house don't count when they're already stinking to the high heavens, and besides, what's to kill when everything's already dead?

So I stood there while Ira threw a match and that was the second time I let Ira decide.

The next couple of years, me and Ira camped out in every hole we could find. Mostly we slept in the back end of the truck but once in a while we'd find an old house with maybe only the windows knocked out and I'd almost think there'd be a momma coming in pretty soon to fix us supper.

We were living off catfish. Sometimes when we really needed some money, we sold the catfish. I never went in with Ira when he done that because people were always asking why I wasn't in school or where my momma was. Or where our daddy was. So Ira said it was better for me to stay at the camp. After a while even that got bad. We were fishing for catfish on this river and we couldn't catch nothing. It was probably just bad timing 'cause sometimes you can catch catfish on almost nothing. A piece of ribbon. A tree leaf. A piece of soap. But the catfish just weren't biting. So Ira said we had to bait the hooks with something live. That's when he started killing all the blackbirds and rabbits he could find and after a while even that was getting hard to find. Or maybe it was just that Ira wanted to shoot something different than rabbits. Anyhow, we had this old cat that hung around the camp. It was an old cat and we fed it scraps and Ira said he was gonna kill the old tomcat and use him for bait. I told Ira not to kill that old tomcat but Ira said he was gonna do it. I don't know why I got so upset about that cat I had never saw more than twenty times, but I kept saying no and Ira kept saying he was gonna shoot that cat and use him for bait. About that time the old tom looked around a tree and Ira hit him right in the head.

That night something hit me. I still don't know what it was, but it felt like a woman's balled-up fist. So I got up and looked around. There wasn't nobody around but I got to thinking, Yes, there is. It was Momma trying to wake me up, trying to tell me something. Ira was gonna kill me or I was gonna kill Ira. I didn't know which. So I hunted down a skiff we had been using sometimes and I rowed to town and never went back.

Fifteen years later, I was sharpening a screw-driver.

SIXTEEN

The double homicide never came home to roost because the Texas game warden agency's policy was: Never Wash Out Dirty Laundry in Public When You Can Send It Out for Cleaning Elsewhere. Or in the Next County. So they transferred Ira into another coastal county to mess with their fishermen and give us some relief. Then too, since Brother Dynamite had gained enough notoriety and dexterity with the snakes that he was invited to private homes and backyards and tent revivals of Holy Rollers as far away as Brazoria County, it was rumored that the brothers might start living together—if they didn't kill each other with a screwdriver first. (Aunt Silver's devil deliverance had failed on me so it probably failed on Brother Dynamite too.)

So I kicked out the screen in my bedroom window and went and told Chief that more than likely we wouldn't be disturbed if we visited a certain river church for a gun. Wasn't that what he was waiting on—evidence of a killer even though the killer was gone? Then I walked back and pried myself through a jasmine vine, trampled on the ripped screen from the window I'd kicked out, and heaved myself through the open window and went headfirst onto the metal bed with its cold chiseled message: YOU WILL DISAPPEAR IN THREE DAYS. Well, I hadn't disappeared yet, but Ira sure had.

I have to admit I was happy about that room that still smelled of my oldest brother who it had belonged to since the room was built, and it had a bed with a worn patchwork quilt and a desk in a corner with a boxy homemade record player minus the records and I had moved that bed and desk on every wall they would fit until I settled on one they wasn't on before. It wasn't cold outside but the room was cool with a blue ceiling that didn't help the coolness none.

Then I sat on the bed and waited while the pale moon spooled outside with a terrible slowness and blotted out shadows deep as a hand's hollow. Then the night got closer and closer and I picked out the dozen dime-sized shapes on the floor where the bed's legs and the desk's legs had originally rested for as long as the room was built. I was asleep before Anthony ever lay down.

Two hours later Chief showed up. He said he was late because he fell asleep in his chair as he did sometimes. Now he just stood there while the smoke from his pipe scoured his face like a rock. I reached under the bed for a pair of my sister's old oversized shoes for my fat sore foot and Chief held the jasmine vine back while I climbed out. Then we both walked down the oyster shell road to Archie Don's truck parked in a ditch full of moonlight.

Hog's Bayou Road. Chief said he'd launched his fishing skiff down that road that one time he switched from chasing black drum and redfish in the bays to hunting catfish and alligator gar in the river. Man, he could remember that. Remembered too coming across the bay in the dead-last hours before dawn with just a compass and a jelly jar filled with black coffee. Heading for the very same bayou. He squinted at the road.

"You hear me," he said.

"I hear you."

"I was a happy man then."

I turned and looked at him. Chief's head was hanging over the steering wheel, his forehead within inches of the windshield and ever' time he approached a hole the size of a quarter, he shoved on the brake pedal, let it out ever so slowly, then crept over the hole like he was trying to keep a sleeping baby from waking up.

"No sense tearing up the truck," Chief said.

The truck's headlights were tearing holes in a tangled mess of oak and hackberry trees and elephant ears and honeysuckle vines when suddenly Chief turned off the key, settled himself down behind the wheel, and motioned with his pipe for me to go ahead.

"I'm the lookout," he said.

"You're also in the middle of the road."

"That I am. But who's coming?"

"I was the lookout last time."

"Yes, you was. But you're ten now. So get on and do the walkin'. And what are we looking for?"

"Archie Don?"

"Pay attention, girl. That gun."

"Oooh."

I stepped out of the truck and it was same as when I was there the last time. Tire marks were still there too, so I turned off on them and beyond the brush I could see the river that was lower than I remembered but clear and unmarked as a girl's hair ribbon. A little farther off the river-bank was the river church in a yard overhung with limbs and vines that blotted out the sky. I headed to the front door and it was open with the same exact dragging edge shoved into the dirt like before. This Jesus crowd was not big on fixing things. I went inside to the window with the bulging screen where I had sat before and the room slowly filled with moonlight like an electric switch had come on inside my head and was burning its way out. I stood still for a second and watched the walls and benches slowly come alive. I walked down front and my oversized tennis shoes slid off my heels and slapped against the rotten floor. There were empty boxes everywhere: against the wall, on the floor and underneath the upside-down shrimp door, on the floor leading to the back room, and against the door. A month earlier I could have pried a lid off any one of them and pulled up a poor misunderstood rattlesnake who was really such a coward that it only struck when its back was against the wall. I didn't know where all the snakes went. Maybe Brother Dynamite loaded them in the back end of his car trunk. Maybe he turned them loose. I wanted to think they were loose and at any moment were free to latch on to someone's ankle.

The back door was open, and besides a half-dozen empty snake cages there was a worn-out chair, a worn-out mattress, and some pants and a shirt in one corner with a pair of mismatched shoes thrown on top. Drabness had doctored everything with its equal-opportunity color because worn-out wasn't bad enough anymore. Then I stumbled on the gun in an unlit corner and it was the only thing not locked in a death grip with rot, decay, and misty river steam.

I picked it up and it looked fine and dandy. Arch's gun. Don't that beat all.

Chief said there were a lot of words out there that stood for nothing. Justice, that's a lotta crap. Sheriffs and game wardens. More bull crap. Preachers claiming to be from God . . . and especially preachers when they're talking over a dead body. BULL. CRAP. That's why Arch needed that gun. Words won't do it. So that's why he was taking me to the cemetery next and I, alarmed and remembering that last time Chief threatened a grave robbing, said, "We're not digging up Arch again, are we?!"

Chief said, "Again? There weren't no again."

"Sure. There was that island. Where you found him!"

"Oh. Nope, not digging up Arch. Trying to get him to lay down is all. Maybe he'll let me lay down if he's laid down first. Ya think he will?"

I said, "Oooh, I don't know nothing about that."

"Well, burying that gun might do it. Maybe it will. Archie Don sure loved that gun."

It was getting close to dawn when Chief pulled up to the cemetery's barbwire fence, and he got out and carefully lowered himself over the fence. Then he held the fence down with his foot while I crawled through. His hands were steady but he let me carry the gun to Arch's grave, where lack of rain had left the grave mound pretty much undisturbed. It looked like a sand dune. Another variation on Baby Brother Sand Dune. Chief probably noticed, too, because he didn't seem to breathe at all. Then he said, "Too bad baby brother didn't have a teddy bear."

"What?" I said.

"Nothing. You can do it there," Chief said.

"Do what?"

"Pay attention, girl. Bury the gun."

No words were said. As Chief said, Words won't do it. Say the word and that ain't it. So we were left to our own devices in that barbwire cemetery and I guess our device was as good as the next fella's, but Archie Don didn't talk so I don't know for sure. Chief and I left after that. It was already daybreak and the sun coming up through a mott of oak trees was splintering into a million pieces. Then Chief dropped me off in the dropping-off place (up the road a piece from home) and I climbed through the window and fell into bed. I didn't dream and I wasn't awake. It was that third thing. Guess it.

"This logo identifies paper that meets the standards of the Forest Stewardship Council. FSC is widely regarded as the best practice in forest management, ensuring the highest protections for forests and indigenous peoples."

The Chelsea Green Publishing Company is committed to preserving ancient forests and natural resources. We elected to print this title on 30% postconsumer recycled paper, processed chlorine-free. As a result, for this printing, we have saved:

55 Trees (40' tall and 6-8" diameter)
19,874 Gallons of Wastewater
38 million BTU's Total Energy
2,552 Pounds of Solid Waste
4,788 Pounds of Greenhouse Gases

Chelsea Green Publishing made this paper choice because we and our printer, Thomson-Shore, Inc., are members of the Green Press Initiative, a nonprofit program dedicated to supporting authors, publishers, and suppliers in their efforts to reduce their use of fiber obtained from endangered forests. For more information, visit: www.greenpressinitiative.org.

Environmental impact estimates were made using the Environmental Defense Paper Calculator.
For more information visit: www.papercalculator.org.

Also by Diane Wilson
An Unreasonable Woman
A True Story of Shrimpers, Politicos, Polluters,
and the Fight for Seadrift, Texas

With a foreword by KENNY AUSUBEL
Paperback • $18 • ISBN 978-1-933392-27-1

"I don't often gush, but this book had me fascinated from the first page and whomper-jawed half the time. . . [A] stunning achievement."
—MOLLY IVINS

"Texas is famous for its tall tales, but they pale in comparison to the true tale of Diane Wilson."
—JIM HIGHTOWER

"Nothing can really prepare you for the nervy, scary, riotous, enraging tale of Diane Wilson's education as an environmental activist—or its ultimately inspiring resolution. Essential reading."
—JOAN DYE GUSSOW, author of *This Organic Life*

"Back in the 1960s there was much banter about who would write the great American novel. Well, I think I've found the book: *An Unreasonable Woman* by Diane Wilson. There's a catch. This isn't fiction. And it's all the more powerful for that reason."
—JEFFREY ST. CLAIR, review in *CounterPunch*

When Diane Wilson, fourth-generation shrimp-boat captain and mother of five, learns that she lives in the most polluted county in the United States, she decides to fight back. She launches a campaign against a multibillion-dollar corporation that has been covering up spills, silencing workers, flouting the EPA, and dumping lethal ethylene dichloride and vinyl chloride into the bays along her beloved Texas Gulf Coast.

In an epic tale of bravery, Wilson takes her fight to the courts, to the gates of the chemical plant, and to the halls of power in Austin. Along the way she meets with scorn, bribery, character assassination, and death threats. Finally Wilson realizes that she must break the law to win justice: She resorts to nonviolent disobedience, direct action, and hunger strikes.

Wilson's vivid South Texas dialogue resides somewhere between Alice Walker and William Faulkner, and her dazzling prose brings to mind the magic realism of Gabriel Garcia Marquez, replete with dreams and prophecies.

the politics and practice of sustainable living

CHELSEA GREEN PUBLISHING

Chelsea Green Publishing sees books as tools for effecting cultural change, and seeks to empower citizens to participate in reclaiming our global commons and become its impassioned stewards. If you enjoyed *Holy Roller* please consider these other great books.

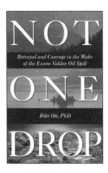

Not One Drop
Betrayal and Courage in the Wake
of the Exxon Valdez *Oil Spill*
RIKI OTT
ISBN 978-1-933392-58-5
Paperback • $21.95

A Language Older Than Words
DERRICK JENSEN
ISBN 978-1-931498-55-5
Paperback • $20

Strangers Devour the Land
BOYCE RICHARDSON
ISBN 978-1-60358-004-5
Paperback • $25

Luminous Fish
Tales of Science and Love
LYNN MARGULIS
ISBN 978-1-933392-33-2
Hardcover • $21.95

CHELSEA
GREEN
PUBLISHING
the politics and practice of sustainable living

For more information or to request a catalog, visit **www.chelseagreen.com** or call toll-free **(800) 639-4099**.